Good Faeries

For Wendy

First published in the United States of America by
SIMON AND SCHUSTER EDITIONS, New York in 1998

This edition published in Great Britain in 2004 by
PAVILION BOOKS

An imprint of Chrysalis Books Group

The Chrysalis Building, Bramley Road, London W10 6SP

Copyright © 1998 by Brian Froud

The moral right of the author and illustrator have been asserted

Design and Art Direction by Fiona Andreanelli
and David Costa at Wherefore Art? London

This is a work of fiction. Names, characters, places and incidents are either products of the
author's imagination or are used fictitiously. Any resemblance to actual events or
locales or persons, living or dead is entirely coincidental.

A CIP catalogue record for this book is available from the British Library.

ISBN 1 86205 3022

Printed in Singapore by Imago

4 6 8 10 9 7 5

This book can be ordered direct from the publisher.
Please contact the Marketing Department.
But try your bookshop first.

Good Faeries

Brian Froud

Edited by Terri Windling

PAVILION

The faeries I draw are a spontaneous manifestation
of my relationship with the world.
A normally invisible domain is given form first
of all in my sketchbooks. Faerie faces emerge from
the blank white pages as if out of a mist.
A few loose random squiggles are drawn,
and suddenly a complete personality appears,
demanding attention and a name.

Preface

ONCE UPON A TIME, I thought faeries lived only in books, old folktales, and the past. That was before they burst upon my life as vibrant, luminous beings, permeating my art and my everyday existence, causing glorious havoc.

Until 1976, I lived in London and worked as an illustrator, creating images to go along with other people's words. Then I moved to a small country village in Devon, along with my friend Alan Lee and his family. As I walked through forests of oak and ivy, across the wild expanse of Dartmoor, among stone circles, Bronze Age ruins, and tumbled stones of old castle walls, I began to hear words and stories whispered by the land itself. I listened to those stories, soaking in the spirit of the land with its wealth of folklore and myth. Together, Alan and I created *Faeries*, a book of pictures and faery lore, which went on to become an international best-seller. This book was considered by many to be a definitive guide to the faery realm . . . but I soon discovered that my journey through the land of Faery had only just begun. I learned that the denizens of that land weren't confined to stories from an age long gone—they were all around me, tangible pulses of energy, spirit, emotion, and light. They took on form as they stepped into my art, cloaked in shapes of nature and myth. I'd attracted their attention while creating *Faeries*, and they weren't finished with me yet.

In the years after the publication of *Faeries* I worked on many other projects, each of them steeped in magic. For Jim Henson, I designed two movies based upon my art: *The Dark Crystal* and *Labyrinth*. I published other books such as *The World of the Dark Crystal*, *Brian Froud's Faerielands*, *Lady Cottington's Pressed Fairy Book*, *Strange Stains and Mysterious Smells*, and *The Goblin Companion* (the last three with Terry Jones of *Monty Python* fame). Yet of all these publications, *Faeries* seemed to have captured the imaginations of the greatest number of readers. When I ventured out of my Devon studio to work on projects halfway across the world, people sought me out clutching well-worn copies of the volume. They were of all ages and from all walks of life, but they had one thing in common: an intense relationship with the book and an immense affection for the imagery within. The faeries had entered their lives, and shaped their dreams, and touched their hearts.

It has been twenty years since *Faeries* was published, and in that time I have never stopped my own personal intensive exploration of the faery realm. During these years I met my wife, Wendy, a sculptor and doll maker, on the set of *The Dark Crystal*; our son, Toby, was born; and we moved to a seventeenth-century Devon longhouse built on Saxon foundations. Faery paintings and drawings began to crowd me out of my studio, spilling into the rest of the house alongside my wife's mythic sculptures, wood-land masks, and faery dolls. My paintings are not illustrations drawn from specific stories or folklore texts; rather, they are images painted intuitively, springing directly from visions guided by faery muses, a paradoxical mix of chance and intent. As

this body of faery imagery grew, I also followed the faeries' footsteps in the study of world mythology, archetypal psychology, and magical esoterica. Through painting, I discovered much about faery nature in a daily, very personal way—and then found these discoveries echoed in myth, folklore, art, and visionary writings from cultures all around the world.

Faeries was a book that concentrated on the faeries of the past, found in old British tales. *Good Faeries/Bad Faeries* is about the magic in our lives today; it links faeries of the past with faeries of the present and the future. I'd always wanted this book to be more than just a presentation of my faery art. I'd also hoped to address the process of creativity and imagination that enables direct communi-cation with the luminous, living faery realm. In folklore, they say that those who can see the faeries are blessed with *second sight*. Where some people perceive only empty fields, a man or woman with second sight can see a host of faeries dancing in a ring or the shining entrance to a faery hill. Where some notice only an ordinary street of shops or a marketplace, others see faeries in human disguise, paying for market goods with magical coins that will turn into mere stones and leaves when the faeries have gone. Through painting pictures and listening to the spirit of the beautiful land where I make my home, I have discovered that the second sight is not limited to people in old folktales. We can all learn to have the sight to see the faery world around us. It shimmers in every autumn leaf and lingers in every cool blue shadow; it gives every stone and stream and grove of trees vibrant, animate life. Second sight can also be called *in-sight:* into the faery realms, into the very heart of nature and into the mystical world that lies deep within the human soul.

In ancient Greece, the word *eidōla* meant image, and *eidōlon* meant soul. Image, then, was a way of understanding and envisioning the soul. This is a book of what I call "imaginosis," or *knowing through image*—a book of images designed to spark self-revelation. Such images grow from my own inner journeys and daily contact with the faeries. By experience I have found them to be irrational, poetic, absurd, paradoxical, and

shifters, highly mutable, for no faery or nature spirit has a fixed body. In their essence, faeries are abstract structures of flowing energy, formed of an astral matter that is so sensitive as to be influenced by emotion and thought. In their most primal form, we perceive them simply as pulsing forces of radiant light, with a glowing center located in the region of the head or heart. (In the more highly evolved faeries, the head and the eyes are more strongly defined.) Responding both to mythic patterns and to human thoughts, these abstract forces delight in coalescing into wings and flowing drapery, taking on shapes that reflect the human, animal, plant, and mineral worlds.

In this book, we explore the nature of faeries in all their various shape-shifting guises. As guardians, guides, godmothers, and

faeries are the inner nature of the land and a reflection of the inner nature of our souls

very, very wise. They bestow the gifts of inspiration, self-healing, and self-transformation . . . but they also create the mischief in our lives, wild disruptions, times of havoc, mad abandon, and dramatic change.

Humans have long maintained close daily connections with the faeries. In centuries past, we've acknowledged them by many traditional names: boggarts, bogles, bocans, bugganes, brownies, blue-caps, banshees, miffies, nippers, nickers, knockers, noggles, lobs, hobs, scrags, ouphs, spunks, spurns, hodge-pochers, moon dancers, puckles, thrumpins, mawkins, gally-trots, Melsh Dicks, and myriad others. Just as they have many different names, they appear to us in many different guises. They are shape

muses, the *good faeries* of the twilight realm are agents of self-growth and transformation, embodiments of the healing energies that flow through nature and through ourselves. Both luminous and illuminating, they reveal hidden aspects of our souls.

Yet as centuries' worth of folklore points out, faeries can also be tricksy creatures, delighting in all things irrational, nonsensical, and wickedly absurd. Did you ever wonder why your socks never match or buttered toast always falls facedown? Did you ever wonder what a Pang of Regret looks like? Or a Mild Panic? Here you'll see the faces and forms of the creatures behind these and darker problems—the *bad faeries* who pinch us, nip us, trip us up, and lead us astray. Yet even bad faeries have their gifts to bestow when we understand their contrary natures. By recognizing and naming them, you'll find they can teach you how to spin the straw of your life into gold.

The pictures that follow were inspired by the dynamic, spirited world around me: the faery creatures who have guided, disrupted, enchanted, and plagued my daily life—pushing, prodding, provoking, sometimes tripping me up so that (flat on my back) I can see from a new perspective. They populate my studio, snooze among the books and paints, flit through the windows, nest in the cupboards, play silly pranks, and offer bright gifts. You'll find them in forests, on mountains, in deserts, on sandy reefs at the edge of the sea; in the gold mist of a country dawn or the silver smoke of an urban twilight; in England and in America . . . and in landscapes throughout the world. Faeries are the inner nature of each land, and a reflection of the inner nature of our souls. They surround me now, as they surround you—you need only the sight to see them.

The pictures in this book all insisted on manifesting themselves on my drawing board. Nothing is made up—these images are direct faery communications. The words I've used to describe the pictures emerged from the same mysterious place, pulsing into and out of focus as though they came to me through distorting glass. This is the way faeries communicate, with high seriousness combined with humor, with symbols, lists, jokes, connections, repetitions, tangents, and deliberate confusions. The smallest figure in the background of a picture might be the most important aspect of all; or an absurd phrase might contain the hidden message the faeries intend. Some faeries demand a complex understanding and mythological erudition;

others express themselves elliptically; still others are deceptively direct. Some words I resisted, feeling they were too obscure or simply ridiculous . . . but the faeries insisted, reminding me that not all meanings are meant to be clear at once. Some ideas take time. Some words are designed to lead us on to inner journeys, with truth hidden deep inside them. In Faeryland, that which seems most absurd is often the key to communication with higher spiritual forces. It is a land where wisdom is inseparable from whimsy and where leprechauns dance with the angels.

This is a very personal book in that you, the reader and viewer, are looking through my eyes and my heart into Faery—and yet it's my hope that these images will encourage your own second sight to develop. Joseph Campbell has said that artists are the "shamans and myth-makers" of our modern world. Like Campbell, I believe in the artist as shaman, journeying deep into uncharted inner worlds, then bringing back sensations and visions encountered in that mythic terrain. I see my pictures as maps of the journeys I've taken through the realms of the soul. And I hope that these maps will lead you to find faery pathways of your own.

Introduction

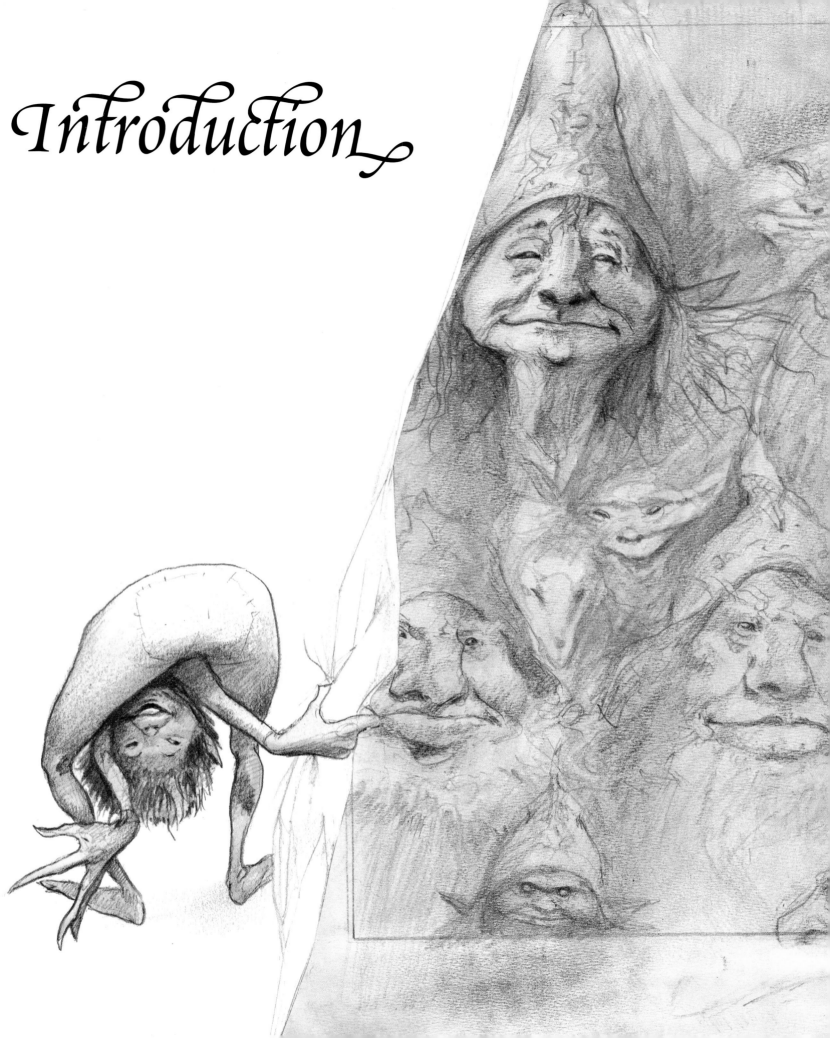

A Note on the Art of Faery

When I paint and draw, I am not concerned with achieving an illusion of depth and perspective. My paintings are like tapestries: flat surfaces woven with the threads of ideas and emotions. It is my intent that the images should be read as you might read a book, the eye moving from one image to another. Beneath the figures and shapes in each painting is a hidden layer of geometry—a framework of circles and straight lines connecting each element of imagery. Thus the paintings can also be read like a map of the heavens, forming patterns of faery constellations; or like a road map, leading the eye from image to image on a winding trail into Faery.

Rather than attempt to provide an exhaustive tour of the faery realms, I prefer to present brief, bright fragments. I like to represent moments, glimpses: Faeryland caught in the blink of an eye or in the instant between dusk and dark. My paintings are full of symbols and signposts pointing the way to the faeries' domain in the hope that my journeys might guide or inspire others making their own. Yet each person's sojourn in Faery is highly individual and unique. Each traveler moves through a very different symbolic and emotional landscape. Thus the true meaning of one of my paintings reveals itself only individually, changing from viewer to viewer.

When painting or drawing, I always try to allow for this ambiguity, for an element of mystery, a looseness, or emotional space, that the viewers themselves must fill. The details of story, feeling, and intent are all supplied by the viewers, not me—and in this way they become part of the picture. I strive for each of my paintings to have a multiplicity of meanings—not only my own, but the meaning each viewer will bring to them. To my mind, a picture is most successful when it enables the viewer to engage in a personal dialogue or relationship, changing from day to day and from year to year, as all things change.

Faery Existence

There is a point in the play *Peter Pan*, as Tinker Bell lies dying, when everyone in the audience who believes in faeries is asked to clap. I, of course, am always the first on my feet, clapping wildly. I believe . . . but too few other people still applaud for the faeries. However, it was not always so—as the evidence of folklore, myth, and ancient history makes clear.

For centuries, since the very dawn of time, the world was perceived as animate and imbued with living spirit. Our earliest art, songs, and stories speak directly of man's relationship with the nonhuman intelligences alongside which we inhabit the sentient earth. Ancient religions both celebrated and regulated these relationships. By learning more about the myths and magical beliefs of cultures all around the world, I have discovered, we gain a deeper understanding of the faery world around us today particularly since faeries communicate to us through the use of mythic symbols, expecting that we (like our ancestors) will understand what they mean.

In early Greece, the Neoplatonists wrote of the Anima Mundi (or world's soul), which mediates between the ultimate divinity and the mundane sensory world—just as the human soul mediates between the body and the spirit. The Anima Mundi is populated by beings the Greeks called daimons, or daemons: nymphs, dryads, satyrs, and all the spirits of air and nature—which are essentially faeries. The human soul flows into and is part of the world's soul; there is no barrier between our essential selves and the world's self. Faeries, being denizens of the world's soul and thus also of our own, exist in both the outer world of nature and the inner world of the mind. I find that although I usually encounter faeries in this inner realm, they can also manifest themselves in startling reality in the outer, physical world—asserting their existence to even the most skeptical of nonbelievers.

Faeries, gnomes, devas, nature spirits, elementals, angels—whatever name we use for them, they were all here before the Age of Reason and they are all still here among us now. It is wise to remember that we deny the existence of faeries at our peril—for they have a disconcerting habit of breaking into our closed worldview, demanding our full attention in subversive and startling ways.

A Note on My Use of the Word "Faery"

IN English the spelling of the word "faery" has been as mutable as the faeries themselves. In early Britain, the Anglo-Saxons would have called such a creature by the name of aelf (elf), yet by Chaucer's time the term "faery" appears to be in common usage. By the seventeenth century we find quite an eclectic array of f-words: farie folk, fairfolks, farefolkis, pharie, phaereis, farie, fairy, fairie, fairye, and faery. While no single name is more "true" than any other, for simplicity I use "Faery" (or "Faeryland") to mean the land itself, and "faery" to refer to one of its inhabitants. The realm of Faery is synonymous with the Celtic Otherworld, the Underworld, the Blessed Isles, Avalon, Tir-Nan-Og, Tir-Nan-Sorcha, the Astral Realms, the Innerworld—all are aspects of Faeryland in shifting, prismatic guise.

The word "faery" originally derived from the Latin *fatum*, meaning destiny or enchantment. This word in turn relates to the Fates, those three omnipotent goddesses who spin, weave, and cut the threads of a man or a woman's lifetime, governing past, present, and future. In Norse mythology, the Fates were called the Norns, or Wyrd (*wyrd* also meaning fate or destiny, hence Shakespeare's Weird Sisters). *Fatum* developed into *fée* (in French) and then into the English "fay"or "fae." An early meaning of faery was "fayerie": the specific state of enchantment created by a fay.

faeries are not a fantasy but a connection to reality

Faery women were once called "fateful women" (*femmes fatales*): desirable, seductive, empowered with supernatural gifts and with an intimate knowledge of the hidden powers of stones, plants, and all things natural. These women were the guardians of special groves, streams, wells, and other sacred places of beauty and power. In the role of muse, they inspired human poets, musicians, and artists . . . and still do so today.

Naming Faeries

I have been painting pictures of faeries and their magical realm for many years now—yet even when their forms emerge vibrant on the paper before me, their names (and personalities) will often remain maddeningly elusive. As I've struggled to find words to describe pictures painted intuitively, I've learned that names, if I'm not careful, can turn them lifeless and flat, nailing the images down to one rigid meaning, lessening possibilities—and greatly dismaying the faeries, those lovers of all things liquid and fluid and bright! The faeries insist on a multiplicity of names, changing from day to day or from moment to moment. Thus the art of naming faeries can be as baffling as the faeries themselves.

I didn't attempt to make names up for the faeries flitting through this book—instead, I waited for the faeries to tell me the words by which they'd like to be known. One stubborn creature's name, for instance, proved to be particularly elusive. He kept telling me that he was the faery of a dead plant . . . and yet he was such a vital fellow I couldn't believe I'd heard him correctly. I asked his name again and again, and always received the same strange answer. Eventually he led me outside to his special spot in my own garden. To my astonishment, there *was* a dead plant there—a beautiful dried *Lunaria annua*, formed of lovely translucent pods. The common name of this plant is honesty. "That's your name? Honesty?" I asked the faery. His reply was a very loud and exasperated "Yes!"

Historically, the naming of faeries has always been a sensitive area. Some ancient cultures alluded to faeries only with euphemisms, either to avoid attracting their attention or simply in acknowledgment of their power. Just as the Greeks appeased the Furies by calling them the Gracious Ones, so our ancestors attempted to pacify troublesome faery neighbors by naming them the Good People, the Honest Folk, or the Darlings—which is rather like calling a big fierce dog "good boy," hoping it won't bite! "*Gin ye ca' me Fairy,*" say the Scottish faeries, "*I'll wark ye muckle tarrie!*" (A rough translation: "Don't call me a fairy or I'll give you a lot of trouble!")

The naming of faeries is complicated by their insistence on mutability; and they themselves change their names according to whim, circumstance, or the needs of the person they're talking to.* Thus a faery I encounter by one name might appear to you in a different guise; or the one who was bothering you yesterday might appear today in a brand-new aspect. Some faeries shout out their names right away ("I'm Arval Parrot!" or "I'm Owling Byrrd!"). Others will tell lies just to amuse, confuse, or test you. Some faeries use temporary names reflecting their appearance (Blue Faery), their place of manifestation (Flower Faery), their function (Faery of Transformation), or their role in Faeryland (gnome). You'll learn other names for these same creatures if you allow a relationship with them to grow. Listen carefully and you'll soon discover the names they want *you* to know.

Despite this multiplicity of names, faeries (like cats) each secretly possess a single real name—usually hidden and guarded, but sometimes given as a powerful gift. The real name of a faery is an integal part of the creature itself. To possess the name is to possess the faery—and it is not a gift given lightly or often. Folklore abounds with stories of faeries angry at humans who steal their names, Rumpelstiltskin (the dwarf who spun bundles of straw into gold) being the best known of them. Discovering the real name of a faery carries with it both risks and rewards. Uttering the name may cause grave offense—or might lead to wishes being granted, certain magical powers bestowed. If the faeries are being troublesome, using their real names might make them desist. But then again, if they are used incorrectly, your troubles might become ten times worse.

Faery Classifications

The classification of faeries is another notoriously difficult science since faeries delight in tricks and illusion, confounding our expectations of them. In this book I have attempted to divide faeries into *good* and *bad*—a convenient conceit for us humans, but laughable to the faery folk. Faeries insist on being themselves, shape-shifting endlessly. Good and bad coexist in some degree in all of Faery's creatures.

Despite the faeries' disdain for rigid order, folklorists, historians, philosophers, mystics, poets, and many others have made numerous attempts to study, define, and categorize the faery realm—if only to make it more comprehensible to humankind. In one basic, worldwide system of classification, the denizens of Faery are divided into four major groups based on the elements: *earth* (gnomes, brownies, and kobolds), *water* (nixies, lamias, and undines), *fire* (salamanders, daemons, and fire drakes), and *air* (sylphs, peries, and all winged faeries). In Eastern philosophy, the classification system is more subtle: there are Golden Devas, who facilitate the transmission of solar energy, or *prana;* White Devas, or sylphs, whose domain is the air; Green Devas, or nature spirits, intimately involved with the growth of plants; and Violet Devas, who create and maintain the etheric structure of all things.

The Anglo-Saxons, like many ancient peoples, classified the faeries by *place:* faeries of the forest and field, mountain and valley, lake and stream. The Welsh divide their faeries into ellylldan (small elves), coblynau (gnomes, or mine faeries), and bwbachod (brownies, or household faeries). The Gwragedd Annwn (the Water Maidens) dwell in isolated lakes, the gwyllion (mountain spirits) haunt the high country, and the Tylwyth Teg (the Fair Folk) can be found in hidden

places. Attempts to categorize Irish faeries produced this list: gnomes, with their large round heads and thick bodies, standing about two and a half feet tall; leprechauns, who are smaller, often bearded, and quite mischievous; the Little People, also small of stature but slender and fair to look upon; and the Sidhe (pronounced *shee*), an ancient race of beings taller than humans and noble in stature, the rulers of the Faery realms (and once of all Ireland).

In other classification systems, the faeries are divided into Trooping (gregarious) and Solitary creatures; or into the Seelie and Unseelie Courts (the former largely beneficent, the latter primarily malign). As useful as these categorizations may be for organizing a folklorist's text, however, in terms of understanding the faeries themselves they'll get you nowhere. At the very core of their being faeries are fluid and transmutable, flowing from one element to another, shifting size, shape, color, gender—changeable as mood or thought. Sometimes they clothe themselves in forms reflecting our own expectations and desires; at other times, it's those very expectations they turn upside down.

For the purposes of this book, I've divided the faeries by their good and bad aspects—and yet, as any pisky will tell you, these are merely two sides of the same coin. We can't expect the faeries themselves to stay neatly put on one side or the other. Faeries cannot be pinned down to a page, a list, a single definition. To grasp their elusive nature requires direct experience, personal engagement. Keep your eyes and your heart wide open. Only thus is Faery revealed.

Elemental Creatures

Having accepted our human need to define and classify even that which stubbornly resists classification, I find

faeries are seen not by the eyes but through the heart

that the most useful way to understand the wondrous variety of faeries is to look at the four elements to which they are aligned: earth, water, fire, and air. Faeries are the physical manifestations of these basic building blocks of creation and the spiritual custodians of all natural phenomena. The following brief catalog gives a sampling of the kinds of faeries you'll encounter in the faery realms, revealing themselves continually in all landscapes and all cultures. Folklore and legends from the past provide us with useful information to help us recognize the creatures of Faery among us today.

The Earth Element

Folktales from all around the globe tell of faery creatures who live deep in the earth: in rocks and roots, in hills and barrows, in caves, quarries, and mine shafts. Gnomes, according to the writings of Paracelsus, can swim through solid earth as easily as fish can swim through water. In Jewish cabalistic tradition, gnomes are said to dwell at the very center of the earth. The knockers are a diminutive race found in mines and quarries throughout Europe, where miners can trace rich veins of ore by listening for the sound of elfin picks. (Whistling, it should be noted, drives these usually friendly creatures into fits of rage.) The Black Dwarves of Scotland, the coblynau of Wales, the gommes of France, the hammerlinge of Germany, the achachila of Bolivia are all varieties of earth-dwelling creatures renowned for being tricky and capricious, but also for sharing their earth-working skills and for sounding warnings in times of danger.

Tree spirits, from the dryads of the Greeks to the Green Men and Women of Celtic lore, are rooted in the earth element, as are all those brownies, goblins, and pixies who make their home among tree roots. Faery women called wood wives run through the forests of Scandinavia; from the front they are beguiling, seductive creatures, but in back they are hollow. In Italy the silvane (wood women) mate with the silvani (wood men) to produce the folleti, who are the mischievous little faeries of that land. The bariaua of Malaysia are shy and gentle tree spirits, while the apuku of Suriname, the saci of Brazil, and the mmotia of the

Gold Coast are far more dangerous to encounter. Kobolds, the hardworking but troublesome household faeries common to northern Europe, lived in trees before they were domesticated, and thus are also aligned with earth.

Ancient earthworks, particularly barrows and other burial sites, are often faery abodes; and hills all over the British Isles are associated with legends of faery revels. The Tylwyth Teg (the Fair Folk of Wales) are said to live under the earth. The Sidhe (that noble faery race) live in Irish burial mounds. In America, little people of the earth live in the trees and under the hills in the tales of the Cherokee, Iroquois, Seneca, and many other tribes. Earth faeries such as these are the spiritual force of nature, reflecting its power, its moods, and its cycles.

Water Faeries

Water spirits can be found in lakes, rivers, pools, springs, wells, fountains, raindrops, teardrops, and at the ocean's edge. They especially love running water in the form of bubbling springs and waterfalls—but any running water can prove to be the particular haunt of faeries. Crossing over (or through) running water is a well-known method of entering their realm.

The nixies are an ancient race of beautiful English river faeries with translucent white skin and long green hair, related to the magical creatures who haunt waterways all around the world—the seductive Nereids of Greece, the playful fenetten of Germany, the enchanting kållråden of Sweden, the dangerous Bonga Maidens of India, and many others. The glaistig is a Scottish goat woman who lives in the darkness behind waterfalls. Strömkarl is a Norwegian faery musician who dwells in waterfalls and is famous for his eleven dance tunes, ten of which he'll teach to humans. The loireag of the Hebrides is another musical water faery— a shy little creature, yet dangerous to those who dare to sing out of tune.

It is wise to be wary of water faeries, for quite a few are treacherous. The ghostly water wraith of Scotland leads travelers to a watery death, and a horrid faery called Jenny Greenteeth lurks at the bottom of stagnant pools. The monstrous Welsh water leaper (Llamhigyn Y Dwr) delights in tangling fishing lines—just like his cousin the ahuizotl, a tormenter of Mexican fishermen, and the Bunyip, a bellowing faery beast at the bottom of Australian lakes.

In salt water, one finds mermaids, mermen, beguiling sirens of both sexes—and the seal people called selchies (also known as sea trows and roane), who sometimes wed human men and women. Saltwater faeries come in guises both malign and beneficent, such as the fierce morganes and the gentle Margot-la-Fée, both from the Breton coast of France. Some sea faeries are known to help sailors and fishermen in storms; others will pull them under the waves even when the skies are clear. Water horses (kelpies), water serpents, and water bulls are other magical creatures bound to the potent element of water, the fluid of life, intuition, transformation, and the depths of the unconscious.

Fire Faeries

Fire is one of the most venerated of natural phenomena, and thus figures prominently in the folklore of many different lands. Various mythological figures are credited with bringing fire to human-kind—usually a Trickster, or Wise Fool, whose own shifting character reflects the dualistic nature of fire, its capacity for great good and great harm. In northern Europe, Loki is the Trickster who steals fire from the gods and gives it to humankind. In New Zealand, sly Maui tricks the fire goddess into giving up all her fingers and toes, which begins a great conflagration. In America, clever Coyote steals fire from the tepee of the Fire People and brings it back to the human world . . . but not without mishap.

In many societies, fire has religious or magical properties, and it is the duty of the priest or shaman to keep the sacred fire burning. In England, sacred fires are still lit on old pagan holy days such as Samain and Midsummer's Eve, always attracting a host of faeries to flitter around the flames. In America, the spirits of the fire can be evoked and honored by gifts of cedar and tobacco; and ritual fire plays an important part in various indigenous spirit-calling ceremonies. Veneration of the fire of the hearth is still common in many countries. In Lithuania, the faery of the hearth is called the gabija, and when the fire is banked for the night, country people petition him with these words: "Dear little fire, dear little fire, you are nicely covered, so sleep, please, and do not walk in this house." There are numerous legends of havoc caused by hearth faeries who have been neglected.

The aitvaras is a fiery household faery well known in Lithuania. Sometimes he is seen in the shape of a flying dragon, breathing yellow flame from his mouth; at other times only his long, flaming tail is visible. The domovik is a Russian household faery and family guardian who lives behind the hearth. He is never addressed directly, but is called Himself or Grandfather. Fire is his special element, and when he is displeased he has been known to burn down the house. If a family moves, the fire in their new hearth must be lit with a brand from the old to welcome this faery to his new dwelling. Supper is left out for the domovik each night to aid him in his busy work of protecting against hostile spirits.

The editor of this book has an English cousin of the domovik living in the old bread oven of her four-hundred-year-old cottage (in the same Dartmoor village where I live). He takes his protective duties so seriously that he tried to chase away tenants when she rented the cottage out during the winter months by scaring them with strange noises in the hearth, creating smoky drafts and an atmosphere of heavy gloom. One day I had a talk with the faery and explained that the tenants were *supposed* to be there—after which, we noted, all such problems in the cottage ceased.

Supernatural smiths are also powerful creatures of

the fire element. Girru, the Babylonian god of metalworking (like Hephaestus in the myths of Greece), represents the purifying aspects of fire as it burns evil away. In Ireland, Goibniu is the divine smith of the Tuatha De Nanann (the faery race), known both for his artistry and for his powers as a magician. In Brythonic legends, Govannon is the master forger and patron of the art. Wayland is a famous smith of Faeryland in many old folktales, renowned throughout the British Isles for the beauty of his faery swords.

Fire faeries come with a variety of names and shapes: salamanders, fire feys, fire drakes, drakes, drachen, and draks. They travel through the air as burning sparks or fiery streaks of intense light, and when they pass they leave an unpleasant odor of sulfur behind. Fire faeries make excellent workers in a farmyard, workshop, kennel, or stable; they will also bring wealth to their masters, collecting gifts and gold from around the world. But these faeries are volatile by

transcendence, flying between the worlds, between heaven and earth, between the body and the soul.

All storms and winds are associated with air spirits, from the gentle breezes caused by faery puffs on the Isle of Man to the great destructive powers of Arabic monsoons caused by angry jinn. In folktales that stretch from Arabian deserts to North America to the British Isles, whirlwinds are the embodiments of spirits, usually up to no good. In Ireland, whirlwinds are made by the passing of whole troops of faeries—and you must be quick to bless yourself lest they carry you away with them. El Numbero (the Tempest) is a Spanish weather faery—an ugly creature in animal skins who rides upon the clouds and causes storms. In Lithuania, a capricious faery called Vejopatis is the master of the winds. A Burmese faery (or nat) called Mbon is responsible for winds both fair and foul. In Finland, ancient Ukko is the Old Man of weather phenomena, commanding the wind and rain, fog and storms, thunder and lightning.

faeries tell us that small things can hold great truths

nature, demanding prompt and proper gratitude. One slight, and a man's wordly goods will be consumed in the fire of their anger'.

Fire spirits, beasts, and faeries reflect the dualistic nature of the fire element. They are embodiments of the destructive and regenerative extremes to be found in nature.

Air Faeries

Air is the element of all winged faeries, whose energies are subtle, quick, and fluid. In mythic terms, the swift wings of thought (and of Hermes) bring messages from the gods. In alchemy, wings denote the volatile nature of quicksilver, an earthly form of the moon's energy: neither solid nor completely fluid, beautiful but dangerous, quicksilver is an earthly representation of a true faery state. Winged faeries are the soul's messengers, representing the spirit freed from the mundane. They are creatures of aspiration and

In America, the spirits of the winds and of the four directions are addressed in the spiritual practices of many indigenous tribes. Ga-ho, for instance, is the spirit of the wind in the Seneca tradition. A benevolent spirit much concerned with the well-being of mankind, Ga-ho lives in the north and directs the four winds, the weather, and the seasons. Wind Old Woman, of the Taos Pueblo people, is a crankier, witchlike spirit—although her husband, Wind Old Man, was even more to be feared. They say if Wind Old Man had not died (or disappeared), the bitter winter winds of that mountain region would be even worse.

The mischievous spirits called gremlins are believed to be modern additions to the faery family, but in fact they are merely new incarnations of flying imps from centuries past. The gremlins discovered human aircraft during the First World War, taking to airborne machines with great delight—to the despair of pilots everywhere. Gremlin sightings and gremlin-caused problems have been reported ever since. Gremlins are unusual, for most faeries despise these big, noisy

machines. Their own method of locomotion is graceful and almost effortless, propelled by thought and emotion rather than the whrrrr of machines or the flapping of wings. And yet faeries are particularly fond of wings, particularly the feathered wings of birds, and sometimes wear birds' wings simply for the pleasure of the aesthetic effect.

Air faeries often take the shape of birds—or combine birds' feet, heads, or beaks with other parts of the human form. The tengu, for instance, are faeries who live in the forests of Japan, appearing sometimes as winged human beings and sometimes as human-faced birds. In the Philippine Islands, the alan are faery spirits who appear half human and half bird, with their fingers and toes reversed. They hang, batlike, from forest trees—and although they can be hostile, usually they are helpful to those in need. Faeries speak the special language of birds, which they sometimes teach to human beings; conversely, sometimes they teach birds to speak as humans do. Some faeries create nests almost identical to the nests of birds, although theirs will often contain bits of silver and other stolen treasures. Faeries have also been known to sleep in birds' nests and to assist in hatching eggs. The cuckoo faery likes to appear in birds' nests just at feeding time, opening his little mouth up wide to snatch a bit of supper.

The flying faeries of the air element are, in general, an evolved faery form, for they incorporate aspects of all four basic elements. The wings of these faeries are symbolic of air, their human or animal legs of earth. A shimmering, luminous quality is their fire aspect; the fluid aspect of shape shifting represents water. Thus they make balanced connections between the four earthly elements and the four directions of the mystical winds. To all these, however, they add the magic of moonlight, the fifth faery element.

Faery Physiognomy

The form of faeries, like everything else about them, is fluid and changeable, for in their natural state faeries exist as pure energy. When we encounter faeries, our minds tend to clothe this energy with forms it can understand. An exchange takes place on the mental level, and the faeries take visible shape in forms derived from location (the trees, stones, or vegetation around them), from our expectations, or from traditional mythic archetypes.* These shapes, though fluid and influenced by the thoughts we bring to a faery encounter, are nonetheless expressive of the true nature of each faery creature. The faeries often borrow details of their appearance from human ideas and folktale imagery: crowns, garlands, clothes, hats, wands, swords, and the like. These too are clues to each faery's nature and the messages it conveys.

The life of Robert Kirk, an Episcopalian minister in the seventeenth century, was forever changed by his dramatic encounter with Scottish faeries. In *The Secret Commonwealth of Elves, Fauns and Fairies* (1690), Kirk stated that faeries are "of a middle nature betwixt man and angel . . . [They have] light changeable bodies, like those called astral, somewhat of the nature of a condensed cloud, and best seen at twilight. These bodies are so pliable through the subtlety of the spirits that agitate them that they can make themselves appear or disappear at pleasure."

More recently, the Irish poet William Butler Yeats (1865–1939) was a man who admitted to many faery encounters. His experiences with Irish faeries seem to have been quite similar to my own with the English faeries of Dartmoor. Yeats stated that faeries have "no inherent form, but change according to their whim or the mind that sees them. You can not lift your hand without influencing and being influenced by hordes" of faeries.

Mythic archetypes and symbols, drawn from stories told for thousands of years, provide the faeries with a potent means of communication with humankind. Faeries are highly mercurial, elusive, ephemeral creatures. Without the ability to ground themselves in the earthy, ancient symbols of myth, these airy beings might simply float away into realms far beyond our ken. The power of mythic imagery allows the faeries to take visible shape and have force here in the human world. When we learn to understand what mythic symbols mean, we learn to understand the faeries.

Faery Wings

Faery wings, formed of shifting light, emotion, and energy, are a manifestation of the power of these beings to transcend the mundane world. Faery wings are not used to fly in the way that a bird or a bee sustains flight, for faeries are self-propelling, borne aloft by emotion and thought. Rather, their wings are a visual expression of the etheric forces flowing through their bodies. "Thought is form" in Faery, so the form of faery wings gives us clues about each faery's function, expressing in miniature the larger cosmic forces at work. The study of faery wings, however, is now a long-lost art.

Winged female faeries are the soul's messengers, representing the spirit freed from the mundane. They are creatures of aspiration and trancendence, flying between the worlds, between heaven and earth, between the body and the soul.

Faery Eyes

Faery eyes can truly be said to be windows of the soul, but it is our own souls they reflect back to us, mirrors of our inner state. This can be disquieting if we are not at ease within ourselves. Faery eyes can seem inhuman, for they are fathomless. Just as the sea is very cold at great depths, so faery eyes can seem cold as they gaze at you from the deepest mysteries of the universe. Yet their eyes can also reveal great wisdom, hilarity, or sorrow—and depths of compassion that are far beyond our mortal understanding.

Faery Horns

Sometimes a faery will appear with horns or antlers curving above her head. This is an example of how faeries express themselves through mythic symbols, for faery horns represent the process of renewal, regrowth, and rebirth. They are also a physical manifestation of intuitive animal powers.

In ancient myths, horned figures are shamanic guides to inner worlds. Cernunnos, the antlered god of the Celtic Underworld (and of nature and wealth), is consort to the Great Goddess, the source of life. He allows himself to be sacrificed each year on winter's darkest day, boiled in her magical cauldron, and reborn with the coming of spring. The horned man, in another aspect, is known as the faery hunter Herne, riding across storm-riven skies with the Wisht Hounds at his command. He is also known as the Faery King, whose tempestuous relationship with his queen reflects all the moods of men, women, and animal nature. He is the lord of animals and the forest, of the cyclical dynamic of male and female energies, connecting us to creative and fecund powers in nature and in ourselves.

Simple, curved, unbranched horns are a reflection of the female crescent moon, indicating a dedication to the transformational processes of the Goddess. When we see horns on female faeries, these are manifestations of their healing powers. Just as the moon dies and is reborn or the horns of the deer are shed and regrown, so faery horns symbolize the cycle of life, death, and rebirth.

Faeries with Red Ears

Red faery ears are the distinctive mark of a supernatural nature. Otherworldly hounds, from the mythic dogs of ancient Egypt to the Welsh hounds of the Underworld (the Hounds of Arawn, lord of the dead, as he hunts in the Forest of the Night), often have red ears. Herne the hunter's fierce Wisht Hounds, who run across Dartmoor on stormy nights, are ghostly white with bloodred ears and eyes like glowing coals. A red-eared bull is the "faery godmother" in a Scottish version of "Cinderella" and a number of similar old folktales. No self-respecting gnome would go outside without his ears buffed to a shining red, and red-eared sprites are the guardians of certain potent, poisonous flowers.

Faery Size

The size of faeries is a hotly contested issue in some quarters. Some faery scholars (who should know better) have humorlessly dismissed the smaller winged faeries as mere literary invention, claiming that the only true faeries are the tall and noble Sidhe. This is nonsense, of course. People around the world have encountered diminutive faeries for centuries—which is why the name "Little People" is constantly used to describe these creatures in many lands and in different languages. Portunes, among the earliest of English faeries, were reported by Gervase of Tilbury to be a mere half inch in height. Brownies are small, gnomes are small, my local West Country pixies are small, but they share the enchanted groves and streams with faeries of every shape and size. Faery scholars would be well advised not to dismiss the "less noble" of faery creatures . . . for the small, common hedge faeries are the true Tricksters of Faeryland, delighting in tripping up anyone who walks with a superior nose in the air and reminding us all to look down every once in a while at the little impulses of nature.

Mystic Heads

When faeries appear, they are often seen in relationship to or partnership with other faeries. A faery crouched on another faery's head indicates a particularly close connection, and the supporting head may symbolize an emotion or represent an outcome. Heads are important faery forms, appearing between the roots of trees or emerging from the midnight shadows and linking us to the mythic resonances that give them such power.

Heads were important in ancient Celtic lore, for the head was considered the seat of the soul. The severed heads of heroes were revered by the Celtic peoples of Europe, as they have been by other tribes the world over. When placed in mystical cauldrons or beside sacred wells, these heads regained the power of speech and become oracular, speaking with the wisdom of the Underworld or the faery realm.

In an old Welsh tale, the severed head of a great warrior called Bran the Blessed traveled and feasted with his loyal companions for a total of eighty-seven years before being buried on Tower Hill, where the Tower of London stands today. Ravens, the special birds of Bran, are still kept at the Tower of London, and it's believed that if the birds ever disappear, the British kingdom will fall. In Italy, Minerva (the goddess of wisdom) sprang fully formed from Jupiter's head—she was the original thought form leaping straight from the mind of God. In old Norse tales, Odin kept the head of Mimir (another wise goddess) to give him magical advice and foretell the future. All over Europe, holy wells were formed where the severed heads of saints touched the ground; likewise, the heads of Mohammedan saints performed many miracles.

Becoming familiar with such tales allows our relationship with the faeries to deepen. When we know that heads symbolize miraculous powers and imparted wisdom, we can better understand the ancient art of faery physiognomy. This is the art of judging character from face and form (*physio-* from the science of the interrelations of matter and energy; *-gnomy* from *gnōsis*, meaning knowledge of spiritual mysteries). Images of faeries sitting or kneeling on gnomic heads are representative of ideas manifested as vibrant faery forms, communicating to us with the divinatory voice of inner wisdom.

The Science of Faery

TRADITIONAL science presents solids, liquids, and gases as progressively finer states of matter. Esoteric science postulates the existence of further states beyond these three, less dense and superfine. It is here that we find the world of Faery.

For many centuries, psychically attuned observers have consistently attested to the presence of *auras* (radiant emanations) around and penetrating the human body. The aura is similar to a magnetic or electrical field: it is a luminous, moving stream of energy reflecting the health of body and spirit. Thoughts, emotions, and physical problems are displayed in the form of color and movement. Various emotions, for instance, can be seen in the aura as a contraction or expansion, or as a particular color or pattern. We refer (albeit unconsciously) to the aura when we say we're feeling blue, seeing red, in a black mood, green with envy, living in a shell, or gone to pieces.

Closer examination of the aura reveals a luminous duplicate of the body called the *etheric double*. This field of energy acts as a bridge between the physical and psychic states. Beyond the etheric is an even finer state of matter known as the astral plane,

faeries are both luminous and illuminating

where our *astral body* receives impressions from and observes the astral world around us. Beyond the astral body is the *mental body*, and beyond this increasingly higher spiritual and intuitive domains. Every thought sets up a motion in the mental body; this motion passes into the astral body, where it takes on form, and then passes on into our physical bodies. Disease has its source in these inner planes and is a manifestation of maladjustments and misdirected force. Thus insights into the astral world are insights into self-healing.

The astral levels are a meeting ground for physical and intuitive states of being, guided by higher cosmic forces. Here, all matter is in a highly receptive state, responding in shape and color to the abstract energies that shape our lives. The human mind better understands these subtle forces when they appear to us in anthropomorphic guise, bringing aspects from the depths of the unconscious or from the higher intuitive planes into our waking perception. When the mind anthropomorphizes these forces (clothing them in mythic, faery, angelic, or other shapes), the image is a doorway to human comprehension: a means of making visible the invisible, of knowing the unknowable, of making universal truths accessible to us. These images are powerful ones, for they are expressive not only of intuitive feelings but also of a divine will. This combination gives these images real spiritual force on the physical plane; it imbues them with vivid, luminous reality in the physical world.

In the astral planes we find a great ocean of universal images that have been produced by millennia of interaction between the mind of man and the cosmic will. The great psychologist C. G. Jung called this inner ocean the *collective unconscious*, a realm containing "the whole spiritual heritage of mankind's evolution, born anew in the brain structure of every individual."* Jung's visionary ideas explain why certain myths, stories, and dreams are held in common by diverse peoples all around the globe. He called these images emerging from the unconscious (or the astral world) *archetypes*. By contacting and working with such images, Jung stated (and the faeries concur), we begin to create inner stability, unlocking the secrets of our soul and, ultimately, of the cosmos.

Faery Communication

I'VE learned that faeries communicate with us in a variety of ways, some profound and some profoundly annoying—including dance, music, mimicry, riddles and pranks, signs and symbols. In communication as with everything else, they exhibit typical faeryness: they are tricksy, elusive, mutable, contrary, and often absurd. I've also learned that humor is very important when dealing with the faeries (or with life itself!). No demon can ever possess us if we maintain the ability to turn and laugh at

*C. G. Jung, The Collected Works of C. G. Jung, *vol. 8:* The Structure and Dynamics of the Psyche *(Princeton, N.J.: Princeton University Press, 1970).*

it. All things absurd, nonlinear, nonsensical, irrational, and madly poetic reveal the secrets of the unconscious and the secret language of Faery.

Wordplay and puns are dear to faeries and demand our true engagement if we are to interpret their meaning. The shapes the faeries clothe themselves in can be considered a kind of language too, holding encoded messages. When we are experiencing any problem, it is wise to ask to see the personified aspect of Faery that is its cause. When we allow that image to rise in our minds, guided by opened intuition, the form it takes will encapsulate the inner truth of the situation. By holding this form in our minds, we may enter into a dialogue with it. The faery will speak to our inner ear or transmit its information by other means: with symbols, shape-shifting transformations, riddles, puns, and absurdities. You must keep your wits about you; hang tightly to the faery's tail for a bumpy ride. Communication with a faery may not be a straightforward proposition, but at the heart of the message faeries bestow, you will find profound truth.

By watching the behavior of faeries, we begin to understand their communication. They speak to us in many, many ways, and we perceive their intent with our ears, our eyes, our hearts—and our laughter too.

Faery Healing

IT is my hope and intent that the pictures within this book may be of active use in engaging Faery's potent transformational powers. I have experienced the healing touch of faeries in my own life and seen what gifts the faeries bestow to those who approach them with open hearts.

From the dawn of time, in various healing practices found all over the world, mankind has viewed itself as a microcosm, or reflection of all creation. In our bodies move the same cosmic forces that drive the universe; our blood moves to the rhythms of the moon, our bones are made of the dust of stars. The human mind and frame embody the ancient mythic principle: *As above, so below.* To understand ourselves is to understand the workings of the universe.

Faeries, too, are primal, natural creatures, agents of the cosmic mechanics that underlie our world. They are intuitive beings, simultaneously in contact with humanity's inner workings and with the inner workings of nature. Like Hermes with his winged sandals, the faeries are fleet-footed communicators, bringing us messages from the depths inside ourselves and from the cosmos.

From out of chaos comes form. From out of darkness comes light. As it emerges from the pure consciousness of the world's soul, a faery coalesces into energy, into pulsing, flowing light. Gradually it manifests itself in a form eloquent of function, molded by emotion. The higher spiritual faeries, or angelic devas (the shining ones), are manifestations of pure thought, giving shape to natural forces and natural processes, and also acting as guardians and healers if we so desire. These higher faeries rarely take an anthropomorphic form; rather, they are experienced as vortices of ever-changing light patterns, a rushing flow of auric forces constantly changing in shape and color in

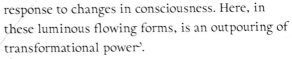

response to changes in consciousness. Here, in these luminous flowing forms, is an outpouring of transformational power.

All things in their primary essence are made up of pure energy, including human beings. Harmony in the body's energy field is essential for health and well-being. Interaction with faery energy forms, especially the higher angelic devas, enhances our vital energies and helps us realize the potential of our own fully functioning forms. In other words, faeries can heal when approached with the proper respect.

By making an active connection with the faeries through these images (as they take on new shapes in your own imagination) you can invoke their powerful healing forces and the healing forces of the cosmos. Each figure and symbol within these pictures is representative of vibrant, mythic, universal truths. Each truth holds within itself an ancient spiritual force. To meditate upon a mythic truth is to connect to its inner power.

Let your heart connect to it. Allow the light to expand into your consciousness. Experience a beautiful golden web of infinite connection, and be restored by pure spirit. At this level of Faeryland there is no dogma; everything coexists, everything is in harmonic relationship, encompassing, flowing, changing, transforming, and renewing.

To engage with this power, stay open, and the faeries here will speak to you. Let them enfold you in faery light. If you desire a specific healing (either physical or emotional), then direct that thought through the imagery to the light energy of the faery realm. The force of this light and energy is powerful on the astral plane; it can be directed outward, to heal someone or something else, or inward, to heal yourself.

Remember, as each man and woman is a microcosm reflecting the larger natural world, so healing of the self is also a healing of the world. As above, so below.

faeries take us to a land where wisdom is inseparable from whimsey, and where Leprechauns dance with angels

Spring, or Primrose, Faery

PRIMROSES are among the first spring flowers, and so this faery leads us into the year as she leads us into Faeryland. Touching the right rock with a primrose is one method of opening the door to Faery. The Irish say that looking over the flowers in a certain way can make the invisible visible, and faeries can be seen.

This frail, sweet flower faery is a messenger from the **Faery Queen** herself, summoning you to Faeryland. She crouches poised to spring into your heart, your dreams, and your imagination.

Helpful Hob

This creature helps in the kitchen, and especially loves baking bread and buns.

Faery Waters of Wisdom

FROM the hands of the **White Lady of the Faery Well** pour the wise waters of Faeryland, sweeter than the finest human wine, smelling of honey and sun-baked earth. Faery spirits have always been associated with wells and springs, mediating the healing properties of water and bringing hidden natural knowledge of the earth to light.

This bright queen pours forth an endless flow of sparkling purity while surrounded by the faeries who cure various physical complaints—arthritis, skin disorders, gout—and a wart faery in very ill temper. Faery wells and sacred springs were considered potent sources of healing by ancient peoples all around the world. Here in the west of England, the old wells buried in the Cornish countryside and the famous Chalice Well at Glastonbury (where the Holy Grail is said to be hidden) are visited to this very day by those seeking cures and blessings. Pins (often bent) were the traditional offering thrown by pilgrims into holy wells—a custom echoed by the modern practice of throwing coins into wishing wells. Rags were tied to nearby trees by those seeking cures for disease or barrenness; as the rag disintegrated in wind and rain, so, too, would troubles fade away.

Of all of the numerous illnesses said to be cured by sacred waters, the most common one was eye complaints. Many votive plaster casts or gold replicas of eyes have been found at the bottom of old wells—some of which were known as *eye wells* in times past. Just as the old meaning of the word "eye" was an opening, so a spring or well is also an opening into the earth and the faeries' domain. Certain pisky wells and faery pools were once renowned as sites of prophecy. The movement of water, or fish in the depths, or the pattern of light and leaves on the surface were all ancient means of divination in England and other lands. At special sites known as *woe waters*, the flow of springs, or lack of it, warned people of war, famine, and other trouble ahead. The **Fountain of Youth** can be found in legends all around the world; in Japan it is guarded by a faerylike creature called **Chrysanthemum Boy**, while in Spain it is under protection of the **xanas**, the fountain faeries.

As we rinse our eyes in this faery well, we open up the eyes of the soul to see clearly and clairvoyantly into other levels of consciousness. The bright queen invites us to drink deeply of the water of Faery, as wisdom flows from the depths of the earth through the **White Lady**'s nurturing hands.

Water Fay

FAYS are the guardians of nature secrets and other hidden knowledge. They rise from the murky depths of water to inspire, enchant, and guide us in the ways of the **Faery Queen**. As the spirits of waterfalls and springs, they pour out healing water to refresh us, body and spirit. Water is the source of our existence, nurtured as we were in our mothers' amniotic fluid. The faeries' gift of pure water is thus a potent one, cleansing and purifying the soul. It is the gift of life.

In times past, the water of faery springs was sought as a cure for infertility. **Fertility faeries**, or **Green Ladies**, could become overenthusiastic in their work, however, enticing men into the woods, leading them on a merry dance, and leaving them exhausted . . . or worse.

The water this faery holds out to you contains the gift of fertility. It may induce fecundity of the spirit rather than of the body, a fecundity of creative inspiration and new ideas.

Oboe Faery

Associated with the expressive, plaintive tones of the oboe, this faery makes an appearance at moments of poetic remembrance.

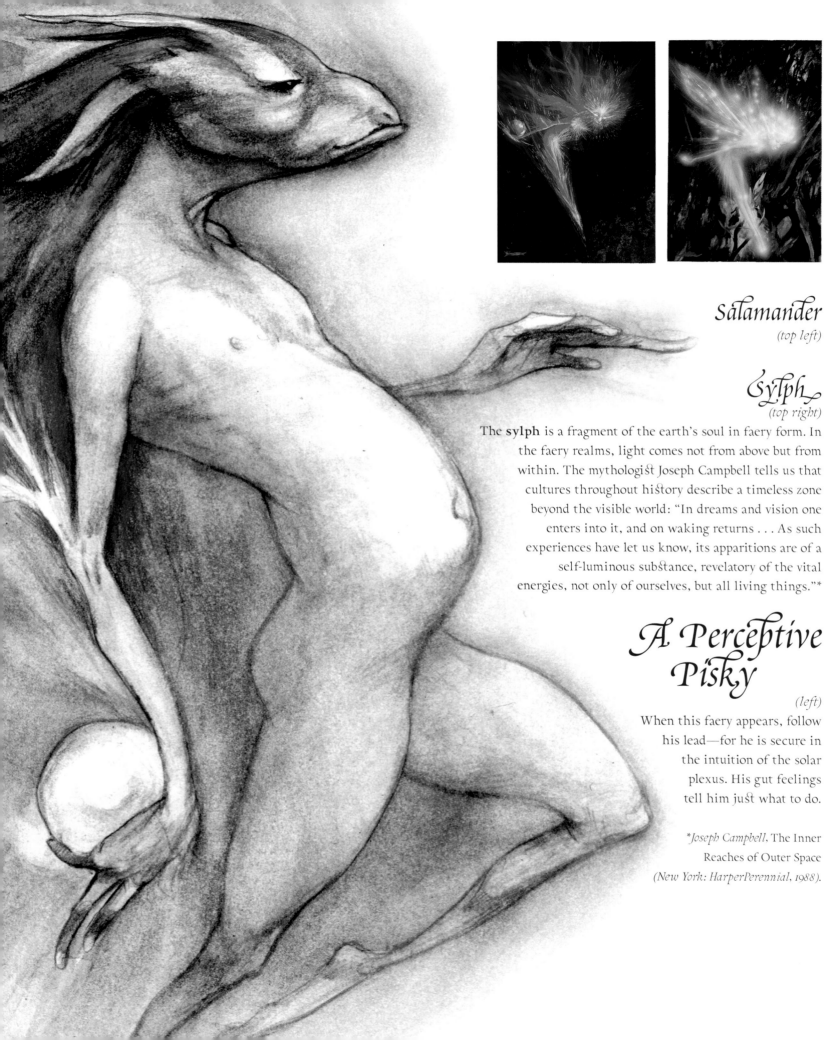

Salamander
(top left)

Sylph
(top right)

The **sylph** is a fragment of the earth's soul in faery form. In the faery realms, light comes not from above but from within. The mythologist Joseph Campbell tells us that cultures throughout history describe a timeless zone beyond the visible world: "In dreams and vision one enters into it, and on waking returns . . . As such experiences have let us know, its apparitions are of a self-luminous substance, revelatory of the vital energies, not only of ourselves, but all living things."*

A Perceptive Pisky
(left)

When this faery appears, follow his lead—for he is secure in the intuition of the solar plexus. His gut feelings tell him just what to do.

*Joseph Campbell, The Inner Reaches of Outer Space *(New York: HarperPerennial, 1988).*

Undine

The Faery Godmother

A Helpful Faery

THE **faery godmother** (or **good mother**, as the Welsh call her) is the faery who brings her special gifts to the newborn. The **godmothers'** ancestors are the **Celtic Triple Matres**, or **Mothers**—who watch over special places such as wells, springs, and the home, and over the course of our lives—and the Greek Fates, the three women who spin, measure, and cut the thread of man's destiny. In Albania, **godmothers** are known as **Fatit**, appearing the third day after a child's birth to bestow the gifts of fate. In Latvia, the **Laume**, a household faery, presides over the three major events of life: birth, marriage, and death.

Godmothers are well-known figures in the fairy tales of many lands, where they mitigate curses, point the way through treacherous terrain, and save inexperienced young heroes from danger . . . and from themselves. In many tales, the **faery godmother** must deflect the curse of a bad faery who feels slighted or offended. In the case of **Sleeping Beauty**, a bad faery was not invited to a princess's baptismal feast. She took great offense and cursed the child with death at the onset of puberty, but the last of the twelve **faery godmothers** mitigated the bad faery's curse. These stories remind us not to forget to invite the faeries to important events. It is wise to acknowledge their presence and graciously accept their gifts.

The moon-wise **godmother** pictured here brings us sacred gifts from the land of Faery. She holds a golden apple from the magical Isle of Apples (also known as Avalon). This glowing fruit of immortality and fertile creativity radiates the rich, penetrating warmth of the summer sun. She also brings us the apple's complement: a crystal of pure moonlight to stimulate clear thinking. With these gifts of the heart, of sun and moon, of male and female in balance, she asks us to place our lives in balance and to find and fulfill our true purpose.

The crescent moon she wears is a symbol of her power. It is a receptacle or cradle holding the sacred seeds of our future—and also a boat in which we can safely sail through the storms of life. Her dazzling halo is made of the bright sparks of faery consciousness. These sparks form a mystical constellation, mapping out our destiny; these are the lucky stars we must remember to guide ourselves by, and to thank.

Leaving us, this **godmother** transforms herself into an owl, a bird of wisdom and farsightedness. When times are dark, she will fly back again to be the good mother each of us needs, nurturing our spiritual well-being.

Guardian of the Sword

WOOD **faeries** titter nervously. Salmon-hatted **pixies** laugh out loud. The lake faery **Lucina** waits by the silver light of the moon. She is guardian of the magic sword forged by the great **Wayland** himself. He also forged her mystic mask out of the world's four elements (earth, air, fire, and water) melded with pure moonlight, the fifth element of Faery. (This is an ancient, sacred art known only to the faeries themselves.)

Lucina wears the white tunic of purity, the blue cloak of spiritual aspiration, and the silver mask of the moon's intuition as she holds the sword of spiritual power. Lake faeries hide these magical swords in their underwater sanctuaries, holding them in readiness for those who may prove worthy. The sword represents the penetrating power of the intellect, held (and balanced) by the receptive feminine. It is not a weapon of war; its blade is intended to cut not through flesh but rather through falsehood and ignorance. In the right hands, the faery sword transforms into the hallowed **Sword of Light**.

Mystical swords are part of the magical systems of many cultures. Sword dances (often with wooden swords or swords made of plaited grass) have long been part of the spring fertility rites in many lands, which represent the death and regeneration of nature. In China, mystical swords call up the wind and emit fire; in Celtic lore, swords speak, bestow the power of invisibility, protect against witchcraft, and cry with sorrow when used in an unworthy manner. Heroes of myth and legend carry magic swords, often forged of faery metals: **Odin, Finn, Sigmund, Charlemagne, Isonokami, Kullervo**, and of course **King Arthur**, who gained **Excalibur** from a lake faery, the **Lady of the Lake**.

Here the faery guardian waits, holding her potent sword in readiness. She waits . . . ready to transfer spiritual power to one worthy of the gift.

The No-Name Faery

This faery came to me one morning, dancing around my weary *head* with his spindly wings, his cheeky grin, spinning a cobweb *crown* of confusion. "That doesn't help," I growled in dismay. *"Try this."* He laughed and teased the crown into long *filaments:* antennas to pick up the waves of artistic inspiration. *Then* he was gone, and I realized that I had never learned his name.

Quempel

(top left) This faery dances to celebrate bright, special moments when something is well done and done well. Then she sits, plump with satisfaction and glowing with achievement.

Vervain Faery

(top right) Flower faeries are what most people think of when the faeries are mentioned—those sweet, butterfly-winged creatures primly populating the pages of nursery books. In reality, flower faeries are tiny specks of light involved with the processes of plant growth at the cellular level. Sometimes, however, they manifest themselves in more substantial forms. Even flower faeries have to grow up.

The **vervain faery** is a particularly vibrant example of the flower faery type. Vervain has always been a plant with mystical connotations. Ruled by Venus, the plant was placed on Roman altars, used at weddings, carried by Roman soldiers for protection and by messengers to signal peace. In Christian legendry, vervain was said to have grown at the foot of the cross. The **Druids** used it in their lustral water for divination purposes. In medieval times it was worn around the head to ward off headaches, poisonous bites, the plague, and even witches, "hindering witches of their will." Vervain has always been associated with the healing arts and has been used to treat migraines, insomnia, and nervous exhaustion, among other complaints. This true faery plant also has diuretic and hypnotic properties.

The **vervain faery** can be called upon for healing, protection, and her general soothing ways.

The Morning Faery

(bottom left) This faery is fond of appearing to housewives and househusbands in the sudden quiet moment when the rest of the family is out the door to school and work. Then she whispers in your ear: "Don't do your chores, don't worry about it. Leave the dishes, the dusting, the dog walking, the dinner planning . . . do something just for yourself right now." She is the faery behind that irresistible desire to read a magazine or a book or maybe to watch a little television . . . but she is also just as likely to urge you to finally write that novel, pick up that oboe, or sign up for that course.

The Knowing Faery

(bottom right) There are no secrets from this faery. She knows where all things hidden are; she can find all things that we have lost. But most of all, she knows what you have hidden in your heart.

The Frog Queen

THERE in the inner realm of Faery, this **Frog Queen** is surrounded by earthy and watery companions: the little impulses of our nature, and one little whim that needs to be pampered. **Pignut the pixie** laughs and says: "She hasn't even got her croak to keep her warm." The others groan and roll their eyes while the **Frog Queen** smiles her secret smile.*

The queen has left her crown and robe behind, for today she's going swimming—in the well of inspiration. Some call it the *well well*, or *healing well*—or the *need well*, for it provides you with what you need. Through our imaginations, we can follow her into the well. Let her leap be yours, and swim downward into the dark and soothing depths.

Many faces peer down at you from the distant surface of the well—faery thoughts and impulses that you must leave behind. Name them if you can, then let them go and leave them at the surface. Follow the **Frog Queen** deeper and deeper, and all you no longer need is washed away. Deeper, deeper, deeper . . . Darkness gives way to a golden glow surrounding you with pervasive warmth as a rich golden light permeates every part of your body, every part of your soul. Rest here for as long as you desire . . . then ask this faery for whatever you need most. Her gift takes the form of a radiant golden ball—hold it to your heart, and its buoyancy will lift you to the surface once more. As you break through to the air above, the ball has become a part of you, radiating faery warmth, light, and power deep inside you. As you emerge from the well feeling light, refreshed, and clear, remember to thank the **Frog Queen** for her help. She will reply that you are welcome to return to the well anytime you need to.

Well, this footnote is more of a leg note—for the **Frog Queen has borrowed the legs of a frog, the most favored and noble of all faery companions. Frogs were known as the healing Lords of the Earth to the ancient Celts of Europe, symbols of good luck and robust good health. They were sacred to **Hekit**, the Egyptian midwife of the gods, representing fertility and rebirth—while **Ch'ing-Wa Sheng**, the Chinese frog spirit, symbolized vision and subtle understanding. Frogs were a sign of harmony between lovers in Graeco-Roman myth; they also represented sensuality and were the companions of the nymphs. Frogs were magical rainmakers in Aztec myths, Aboriginal lore, and the folktales of many African peoples. In European fairy tales, the frog or toad was an agent of transformation: princes hid in frog disguise and frog wives conjured magic of the heart. In alchemy, the jewel concealed in the toad's head symbolized spiritual truth—reminding us that outward appearances can be deceptive and that hidden rewards can be found in the most unpromising material or events.*

Altheia, Faery of Revelation

Altheia uncovers the nature of life, pulling aside the world illusion to reveal the hidden truth within. Call upon this faery for protection against deception and fraud.

Queine of Pharie

In sacred groves and ancient orchards, the **Queine of Pharie** passes on the old year to the new in the form of autumn fruit. Just as this year's apple contains the seeds from which new trees will grow, hers is the gift of past knowledge given to create future potential.

Moon Sphinx

This sweet-dream moonbeam maiden is a faery of new beginnings. The child of **Epona**, the ancient Celtic moon and horse goddess, she guides us through darkness and light, through all the moon's deep mysteries, into the faery realms. Her bright wings speak of spontaneity, freedom, and the swiftness of thought, while her knee rests on the old magic of earth formed of soil and stone. In the human world, it is the gold heat of the sun that germinates seeds, but in Faery the psychic seeds of growth are nurtured by the moon's silver light. The moon waxes: it is the maiden's time. Call on her for guidance through the dark.

The Dawn Faery

(top) Bodysurfing on solar wind, she radiates confidence and helps at moments of self-doubt.

The End-of-the-Day Faery

(bottom) Soaring in the sun's last rays, this faery lives in the joy of past memories, yet moves through the growing darkness toward a bright tomorrow. This faery is beneficial at moments of crisis or of great loss.

The Sphinx

At night, when worry keeps me awake, the faery **sphinx** appears, luminous and perfumed in the darkness. At all moments of daily decision making I find that she is also present. *What is the best thing to do? What path should I take? Should I—yes or no?* These are the urgent questions I ask her—but she'll answer only when she chooses. The faery **sphinx** is very proud, for her lineage is aeons old.

As an aspect of the moon goddess, the **sphinx** is a custodian of primal secrets, full of questions, riddles, rhymes, and clever tests of initiation. She crouches on an owl,* a sacred bird of the night and symbol of the moon. Opposites are brought together and united in this faery's powerful form; thus she unites and mediates between the upper and lower worlds, combining animal natural impulses with the human rational intellect. Untamed and free, the faery **sphinx** is poised at the crossroads of our lives, speaking in riddles, demanding that we know the answers that lie beyond. The **sphinx** is the dark destroyer of all old patterns and outmoded ways of thought—and yet she is also the creator of new insights and new directions. She awakens our sleeping potential with her sharp gaze, her riddles, and her roar. She guides our path into Faery with the radiance of her wings.

*In the folklore of many cultures, the owl is the spirit guide to the Underworld, often associated with the Goddess, an embodiment of her wisdom. **Minerva, Lilith, Blodeuwedd,** *and* **Athene** *all claim the owl as their totem bird; and early Sumerian moon goddess figures have the all-seeing eyes of the owl. There can be no lies before its gaze piercing through the black of night and deep into our very souls. The owl brings penetrating, sometimes ruthless wisdom to bear upon our lives, along with moments of illumination and prophecy. As a bird of death, the owl symbolizes transformation and profound change.*

Bright Shadow

This radiant being fights the street shadows of drugs and menacing violence, illuminating dark alleyways with the light of her compassion. She is a stalwart companion in moments of crisis or physical danger.

Expression Faery

This faery helps in modes of expression such as dance and body posture, and with skills such as cooking, writing, acting, drawing, and making love.

Grig

The word *grig* means something small, and in this case refers to apple-tree faeries. **Griggling** apples are the small apples left on the trees for the faeries at harvest. These apples eventually fall to the ground and ferment into an intoxicant. The **Little People**, like the birds, greatly relish this natural cider, which is no doubt where the expression "Merry as a **grig**" first came from.

Small Woodland Faery

The welfare of all little furry creatures is this faery's daily concern.

Arval Parrot
&
Owling Byrrd

Arval Parrot lives at the base of a tree (his brother, **Owling Byrrd**, above, lives higher up) and takes a special interest in the welfare of birds—owls in particular, but also any bird with a distinctive cry or song. This **gnome** is very helpful to humans with throat problems. Although he didn't show us today, there is something odd about his elbow, but they are one of a kind⸮.*

*As I wrote this, **Arval Parrot** insisted that his elbows were two of a kind. "Two-two," he cried, "twit-to-wooo, twit-to-wooo; your daddy did a poo; your mommy kissed a stranger and stuffed him up the fluuuuueeee." He then sang the old faery song "Forty Fousand Feathers on a Frush's Froat" and added that if I need to know more on the subject, I should consult his brother.*

The Faery of Pure Joy

This luminous creature is the best-loved faery in all Faeryland.

The Mask of Truth, True Dreaming

(overleaf) It is midnight, and the faeries are gathering. The **Faery of Aspiration** welcomes us with upraised hands into our spiritual potential. Dour **gnomes** watch from the shadows, called from the deep regions of the earth. **Silvanus**, guardian of the woodland and its creatures (a faery of physical fecundity and fruitful thought), holds the golden-winged emblem of spiritual journey. This mask, decorated with the wings of **Hypnos**, facilitates the understanding of dreams, deep thought, and meditation. It is a mask of truth, for to wear it is to look inward—toward a true reflection of yourself. Yet some of us can bear to hold the mask for only one brief glimpse.

   The faery **Kundrun** holds one of the many sacred swords of Faeryland. This one, forged long ago by mysterious dwarves, is laid across the cliff of the Otherworld as a bridge to Faeryland. The two-edged sword symbolizes the union of the human world with the world of Faery, as well as the union of the outer world of nature with the inner world of the psyche. It is the sword of clear-cut understanding and sharp perception. But once we cross into Faery it becomes the sword of courage and noble service.

The Faeries of the Future

(overleaf) In Faery, past, present, and future are deeply intertwined. The **Gnome of Now** looks in both directions, backward and forward, at the same time. He knows both Then and Now (particularly Now), but he says nothing. Other **gnomes** urge us onward: Anna steps forward, carrying the hazelnut of wise future choices; Puggi kneels* expectantly, ready to leap into flight. These are the faeries of a bright future and are essential companions on any journey. When these faeries appear, it is time to consider where we have been and where we wish to go.

Many faeries in this book are pictured in the act of crouching. This is because they are poised in a state of potential—ready to leap in any direction, or in another form. They are caught in the act of becoming.

THE FAERY OF PURE JOY

THE MASK OF TRUTH

THE FAERIES OF THE FUTURE

Argea, the Fateful Faery

In twilight by the river's edge waits the faery queen of fate, **Argea**. Ancient Irish bards believed riverbanks were sacred places of revelation; it was there that *eisce* (wisdom, inspiration, and divination) could be gained. Between the flow of water and the fixed element of earth, the numinous **Argea** reveals what has gone before . . . and what will be. Your fate is in her hands.

The Rainbow Faery

Guarded by her **gnome** king, **Iris the Faery Queen** offers her rainbow magic to **pixie** archers. She appears in the middle of dark storms to give us hope—reminding us that hope can soar as far as the **pixies'** rainbow-tipped arrows.

Poetic Pan

THE name **Pan** means all or everywhere—and like many faeries, **Pan** can materialize simultaneously in many different places. This little **Pan**, for instance, appeared to me in the shadows by a woodland stream. Contact with the **poetic Pan** causes erotic impulses, abandonment to poetic emotions and to intense feelings of spiritual connection to nature. Be careful when you call on him, for his influence is overwhelming.

Flow Faery

This faery is the **Director of Dreams**, manipulating dream images and emotions. He specializes in lubricating the free flow of creative ideas. I've found that some days he prefers to stay in bed, leaving us humans stuck.

The Dressing of a Salad

IN Faery, secrets are whispered in the shape of a wing or a faery's hue. This blue prince practices the art of balance: the balance of head and heart, of passion and intellect . . . all manner of balance, including the balance of flavors in fine cooking (cordon bleu, of course).

The faery creature above him is also an agent of balance, harmony, and savory flavors. Her tail gives her equilibrium and her wings are about to unfold in a spiritual flowering, while her froggy feet swim in the deep waters of the unconscious. She holds an embryonic idea, one that is still undetected at any conscious level. The faeries like to bounce and play with these resilient astral spheres. Sometimes in the midst of a game the spheres collide, instantly forming a fully realized creative thought. We've all had that experience, when inspiration comes out of nowhere.

As the ancient Celts knew, our inner selves and the world of Faery are one and the same. Faery is a land of paradox, being both outside and within us. It is a timeless land, existing simultaneously in the past and in the future. The Faery domain contains and creates form, yet it is limitless and amorphic. All opposites achieve balance in the perfect "now" of Faery.

These two faery creatures teach us the metaphysics of balance, a process resembling the creation of a good salad dressing, in which oil, vinegar, and herbs coexist in balanced harmony.

This good faery brings the gift of light and love from the divine source.

The Good Word Faery

Gwenhwyfar

S H E is the **White Shadow**, dancing by moonlight to the faery piper's tune, leaving tiny white star flowers to glow where her feet have trod. She dreams that she dances among constellations far beyond our knowing.

Faeries love to dance. Their music is the most haunting music ever heard by human ears, sad and sweet, deeply sensual, tranquil one moment, demented the next. The **White Ladies** are luminous faery creatures who dance by the light of the moon, beautiful as the music itself, trailing patterns of color and mist in their wake. Faeries often dance in circles, leaving rings of flattened grass to mark the sites of their midnight revels—or circles of toadstools springing up where faery feet have trod.

Faeries dwell in the twilight, between day and night, between spirit and matter, between the conscious and the unconscious . . . where all things are possible, where our past and future meet, where we meet ourselves coming back. When we dance with the faeries, we dance with the reflections of our true selves and the true inner self of the world.

Dream Weaver

(*overleaf*) Here is **Penelope**, my dream weaver. Sitting on a stool at my drawing board, she is my creative guide into the faery realms. Starlight shimmers around her, a visible form of the cosmic energy patterns that flow through everything. At the luminous point where inspirational energies (focused downward from the heavens) and nurturing energy (focused upward from the earth) meet in harmony and balance, **Penelope**'s faery form springs forth, spirit manifest as matter.

We talk of intelligent or gifted people as being bright or dazzling. We say we have a bright idea, a flash of intuition; or we speak of gaining enlightenment. When we look at faeries, we see all these things made visible in glorious form. **Penelope**, like all faeries, is luminous (self-illuminating, a revelation of the self). She is a bright vessel of natural wisdom and exquisite faery grace.

By calling on this faery's help we create focused energy and open ourselves up to higher intuition. She shows us how to reconnect to heavenly and earthly power. Take the glowing gift of inspiration she holds out to you to guide you on your journey, leading to all that you might be. And remember, like this faery, to keep a light and open heart—for self-illumination is the brightest light of all.

Laume

(*overleaf*) A Lithuanian faery, the **Laume** exhibits typical faery traits: she appears naked, likes to bathe, and is known to help orphans and the poor. She spins, weaves, and (like the three Fates) rules over the fate of men. In Latvia, she goes by the name of the **White Lady**. Here she sits and dreams of the stars . . . while this **gnome**, too, has his mind on higher things.

Laume knows that there is no star too far to reach, no dream that may not come true. She's the faery who'll help turn impossible goals into shimmering reality.

GWENHWYFAR

DREAM WEAVER

LAUME

The Faery of Transformation

The touch of this faery's wand brings clarity and a certain transparency. Like this faery, we become transparent to ourselves, able to see that every inner space and corner is clear, bright, free from hidden agendas or distorted motivations. Above the temple of the Delphic Oracle and on the portal to Faeryland are carved two words of magic and power: "Know thyself."

The Faery of Intuition

This faery takes the form of synthesis between animal instinctive nature and the higher nature of the intellect. Her forehorn indicates the penetrating powers of insight and intuition. She is the leap of faith into a brighter future, borne on wings of higher consciousness.

Liminal Lady

(left) "Liminal" (from the Latin *limen*, meaning threshold) refers to the psychological state of transition. All faeries appear on the threshold of what is and what is to be. Call upon her in times of change—or when change is needed but not forthcoming.

The Truth Faery

(middle) Mediating between us and the world's soul, this radiant being lets the bright light of wisdom illuminate our darkness.

Emerging Faery Form

(bottom) **Emerging Faery Form**

Queen Brighid the Bright

Queen Brighid the Bright comes to light out of the darkness, stepping from **Tir Tairngiri** (the Land of Promise) to whisper old magical tales in our ears. In her hand is the white wand of authority once wielded by the old kings of Ireland and the old lords of the Scottish isles. The white of the wand represents purity; its straightness represents justice. Made of stripped birch or willow, it brings the light of spring to the dark of winter. To be touched by this faery's wand is to be given the gift of firm resolve and true purpose on your spiritual journey. She stands in the space between *now* and *know*, initiating all who desire into the mysteries of Faery.

The Retriever

You meant your golf ball to go straight down the middle, yet somehow it veered into unknown terrain. Not to worry. This watchful faery has it safe in hand.

We all occasionally throw our precious hopes and dreams into the universe, where they seem to disappear without response. The **Retriever** is holding on to them in what he calls the **Lost Property Office of Unclaimed Wishes**. Sometimes our purposes and plans do not follow the course we want them to take but are held instead in safekeeping until the time for them is right. Trust in the universe, and in this faery who has your best interests at heart—but don't forget your claim ticket, or your dreams may be lost forever.

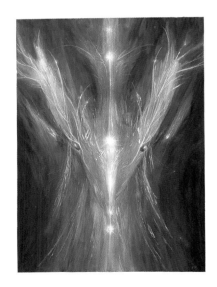

Faun

This **faun** dwells in a sycamore tree in my garden. He says his name is **Biag**.

Honesty, the Faery of the Soulful Eyes

In this faery's gaze, we see that eyes are truly the mirror of the soul. His eyes reflect *our* souls and hearts: we can hide nothing from him. The **honesty faery** is not a judgmental or accusing creature, but rather is empathic, compassionate, able to see through all our convoluted motivations to the heart of any matter. Summon his help when you need clarity, particularly when your motives are unclear. He teaches us compassion for ourselves and asks that we learn this lesson well— for only when we are honest, clear, and loving to our own spirit can we give these gifts to others.

This faery is always honest, however, so summon him with care. He won't tell you that hideous necktie is fine; he won't assure you that no one will notice a botched haircut or a gain of twenty pounds. He's not the faery to soothe your pride when you've made a stupid or embarrassing mistake. If it's an honest opinion you need, then this faery is the one to ask—but be prepared for the plain, unvarnished truth in those soulful eyes.

Ghost of a Mushroom

This creature said it was a **ghost of a mushroom** . . . but what it actually meant was that it is part of the process of physical decay and transformation.

The Plymouth Rock Faery

One of the mysteries of faery communication is that sometimes faeries will tell us things that do not make any logical sense (at least in earthly terms). This faery insists that he lives in Plymouth Rock, where the Pilgrims landed, and also in a rock under the Statue of Liberty. He refuses to clarify this message. I can only assume he functions as some sort of intermediary helping immigrants or visitors to American shores.

Angel of Spiritual Empowerment

ANGELS are the thought forms of God, and heavenly messengers. (The word comes from the Greek *angelos* and the Latin *angelus*, meaning messenger or courier. The Sanskrit *angras* means a divine spirit.) They are the form builders of the universe and embodiments of divine will, perched at the top of a continuum of spiritual beings flowing downward to the smallest of faery creatures. **Angels** could be called grown-up faeries . . . or to put it another way, faeries are little angels.

The hierarchy of angels and their various functions is extremely complex. There are angels of healing, angels of music, angels of peace and blessing, angels of growth and nature, angels of beautiful places, angels of countries, and many, many others. All phenomena of thought or emotion that are subjective to us are objective to angels. Angelic emotions, aspirations, and consciousness are all external, visible, pulsing and flashing through their bodies. The exquisite beauty of angelic faces is due to this: these beings are literally open and transparent, revealing pure intent.

All angels mediate cosmic and spiritual forces and will come to our aid when we call upon them. The **Angel of Spiritual Empowerment** is a particularly radiant creature. Ask for his help as you embark upon your spiritual journey.

Guardian at the Gate

(bottom left) When my son was young, every morning I would stand with him at our gate in a leafy country lane, waiting for the bus to school. It seemed to me that our quiet road led (via ever-larger roads) into the whole wide world beyond. Turn left and you might end up in France, or in America; turn right and you might end up in Africa or Japan . . . or maybe just the village shops. Each morning as I waved my son off to school, it seemed I was also waving him off onto the larger road of life. And so this time at the gate each morning became a time of prayer.

I prayed for his day, for his future, and for the future of children everywhere. I prayed that our little country lane might indeed be the safe beginning of a pathway into a brighter world. And over the years I became aware of a shimmering form above us, radiating pure energy down onto the garden gate. It seemed to bless my son and all who walked in or out of the gate, as well as guarding us against any who would do harm.

Partnership

(bottom right) Spiral energies flow upward and downward in a dance of tension and resolve, flux and form, masculine and feminine moving in perfect harmony. This faery facilitates partnerships in work, play, love, art, and all other aspects of life.

faeries embody the profound abstractions that heal and transform

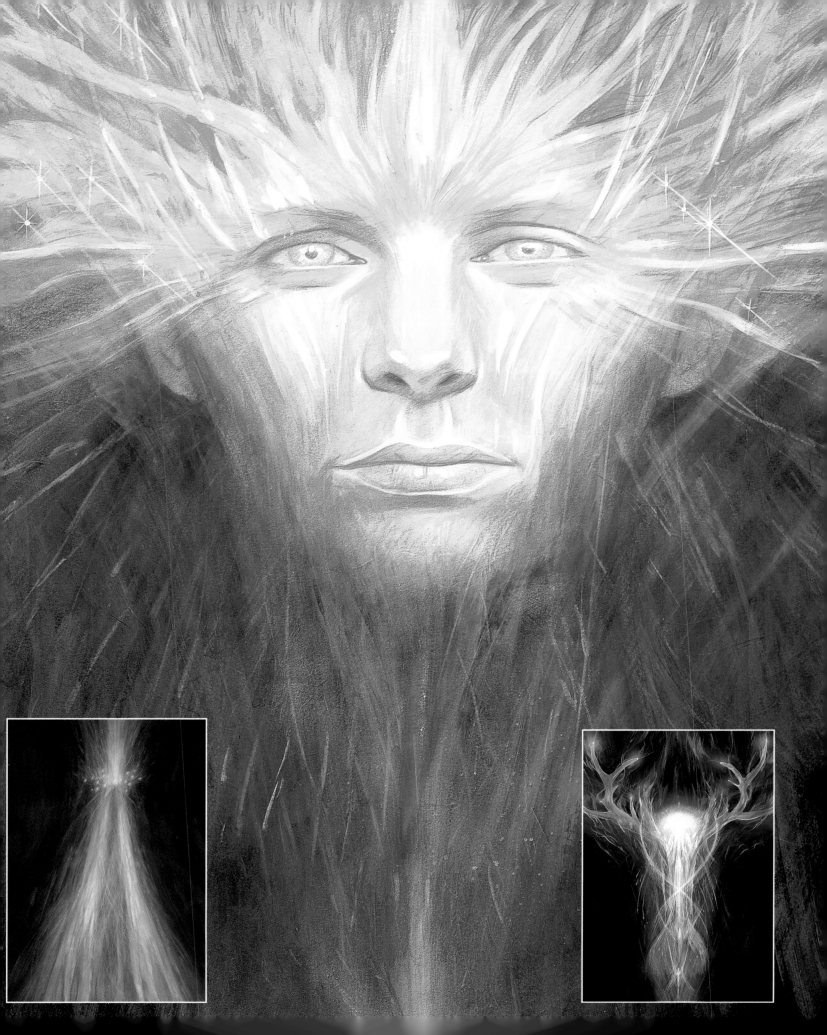

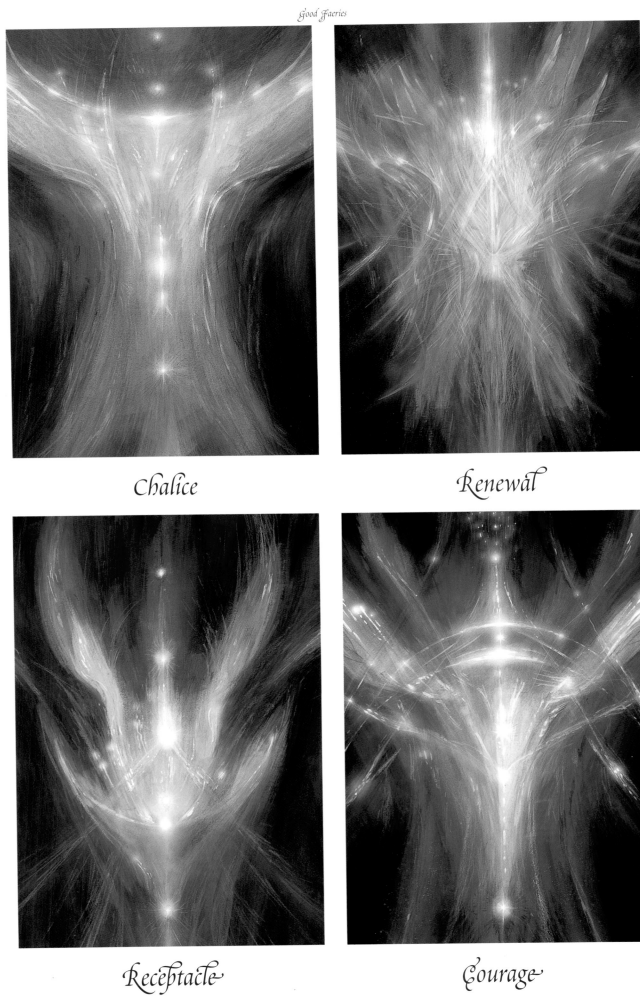

Chalice

Renewal

Receptacle

Courage

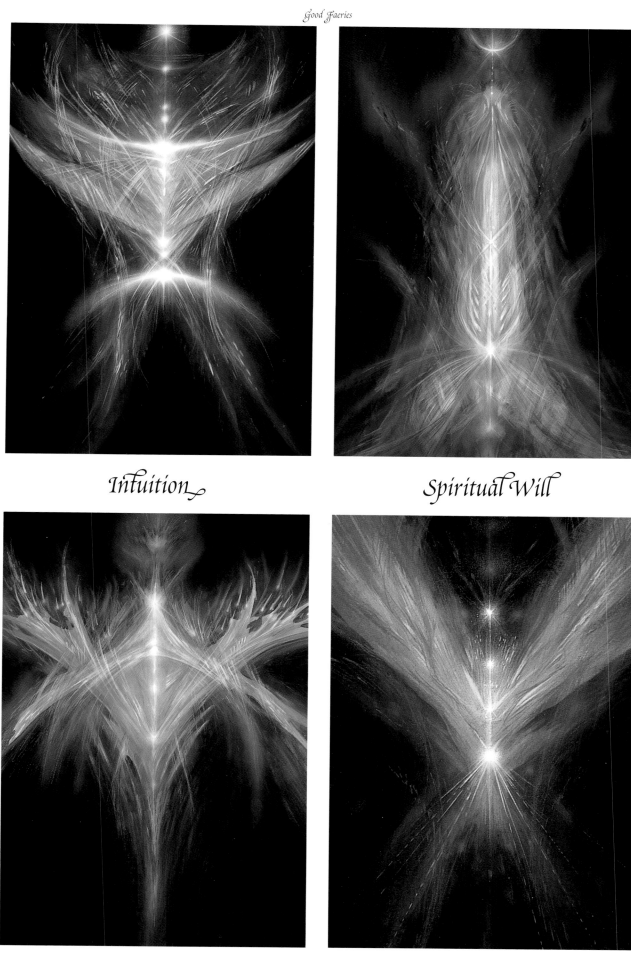

Intuition

Spiritual Will

Connection

Transformation

Gladfly

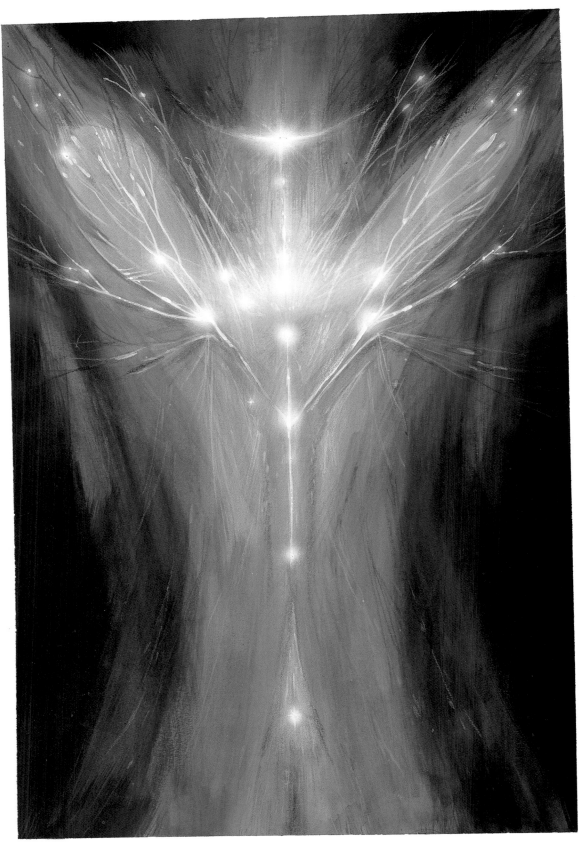

A spirit that joyously dances in the moonlight on the surfaces of lakes and ponds.

Healing Goddess

This lady is the archetype of the **Great Goddess** of regeneration and healing. The blue auric forces surrounding her radiate the universal love we came from and will return to. Call upon her for healing of the body, soul, and spirit.

The Green Lady of the Faery Knoll

A CCORDING to a Gaelic story, the **Queen of Faery** (the **Green Lady**) felt sorrow for the foolishness of the world, and so she invited all women to come to her knoll to be given wisdom. Many women disdained to come, believing they knew better than the faeries already. But other women trooped to the knoll to hear what she might say.

The **Faery Queen** appeared before them, holding the **Copan Moire** (Cup of Mary), in the form of a small blue limpet shell. "In this cup," she said, "is all the world's wisdom, which I will share with you." Some of the women laughed at this, turned around, and went home. But others remained to drink from the shell—which is why to this day some human women are foolish ("no better than the men," as they say) and some are very wise.

A "child of the knoll" is a wisewoman whose practical good sense comes from a deep rapport with nature. The **Faery Queen**'s limpet shell reminds us that small things may hold great truths.

A Faery of Focused Attention

(above, held by the pixie) This beguiling faery creature aids in concentration. I have found that she is very flighty and it is difficult to persuade her to stay for very long.

The Green Woman

From high in the roofs of cathedrals and churches, the ancient **Green Man** stares down at us, a pre-Christian spirit of vegetation carved in the form of a foliate face disgorging leaves from its grimacing mouth.

Less well known is the **Green Man**'s secret companion, the powerful **Green Woman** (or **Sheela-na-Gig**), a fecund, feminine spirit expressive of nature's spiritual power. This irrepressible earth spirit is depicted in the old stone carvings disgorging leaves not from her mouth but from between her legs. Her time has come. Her laughter is free and wild, ringing through the woods.

A Berryman

Seen mostly in the autumn, this faery watches over the ripening of berries. Call on him for help in bringing projects to conclusion. He seems to be receptive to this doggerel:

Tiddymun, Tiddymun,
my story's begun.
Now let it end
well done,
well done.

The Weed King

(*opposite*) This faery oversees the growth and general well-being of the weeds that are abundant in my garden, reminding me that "good" and "bad" can be the same thing. A large thistle in a vegetable patch would be a weed to most gardeners, while to a goat it is a gourmet meal. The **Weed King** radiates qualities of determination and purpose. His tenacious vigor permeates the plants that grow in inhospitable terrain or on fringes and edges, giving succor to wildlife. Call upon him for tenacity, determination, and vigorous health—or when you need help to see the good in the bad (or the bad in the good).

Plant Sap Faery

(*opposite, bottom left*) The **plant sap faery** is a facilitator of growth, for he directs the moisture bathing all the cells of a plant. These faeries are responsible for the rich greening of nature.

The mystic abbess **Hildegard of Bingen** (1098–1179) used the word *viriditas* (greening) to convey a sense of moist, creative fruitfulness. She said that the soul was the moisture of the body, and urged all to be "wet and moist, green and juicy." The **sap faery** represents the rising fluidity that allows all creativity on every level. He is there at openings and beginnings, an embodiment of expressive spontaneity and emotional openness. Call on him at the beginning of creative endeavors (such as artistic work, cooking), at the start of a new course of study, or job, or love affair—or else at the end of an endeavor, when you are tired, emptied out, in need of restoration and renewal.

Plant King of a Field of Barley

(*opposite, bottom right*) The **Barley King** oversees the growth and order of the barley fields. He "dies" when the crop is cut, is absorbed back into the green consciousness of the land, and is reborn in the spring. This faery embodies aspects of the great cycle of death and regeneration.

A Myomantic Gnome

(opposite) This creature says he's a skilled practioner of myomancy, the art of divination through studying the movement of mice . . . and I'm sure it's true.

A Wayside Gnome

(below) He claims he is an expert in phyllomancy, the art of divination through the rustling of leaves . . . but I'm not sure I believe him.

Gnome

(above) **Gnomes** live in the ground and are famous for their stubbornness and their wisdom. **Gnomes** are practical, down-to-earth, deeply rooted in reality, and disapprove of anything airy-fairy. Unfortunately, a **gnome** is also prone to being a stick-in-the-mud and can get bogged down with inertia. The thoughts of the **gnome** tend to be very precise . . . but also very slow. A sentence might take a whole year to speak (or in the case of certain gnomes, an entire century). **Gnome** jokes are not very funny because they never get to the punch line.

The King of Green Men

THE realm of this noble king is **Ytene** (now known as the New Forest), where he rules over the vegetative life forces of an ancient woodland in which humankind and nature have worked in cooperation for countless centuries. It is his role to regulate this relationship, maintaining a harmonious balance in the husbandry of the forest. He keeps a stern but fair eye on the medieval rights of pannage, turbary, and estover, whereby humans enter the forest to graze their pigs on acorns, cut turf, and gather firewood. He has watched **Ytene** since primordial times: he has seen saplings grow into huge trees that have long since decayed, nurturing new growth; he saw **William Rufus**, king of England, killed by an arrow in 1100. It is he who watches over the grazing deer and horses.

"To be wood," in medieval terms, meant to undergo a period of wildness, even madness. In a shamanic rite of initiation similar to practices found all over the world, **Merlin** disappeared into a Welsh forest after the battle of **Arderydd**, where he lived like the deer and wolves and eventually learned the speech of animals. Going into the wood alone, living as the animals live, helps us to understand the spirits of the wilderness and our own wild nature.

The **Green Man** is a very ancient figure, found in abundance in Celtic countries (carved into old stonework and wooden timbers); he is also known all over the world in his guise as a vegetation god. In Finland he is **Metsänhaltia**, the ruler of the forest—an old, old man with a long gray beard and a coat made of lichen. The **Green Man** is a powerful, wild synthesis of man and nature, the vegetative counterpart of humans, the hidden green aspect of mankind.*

Theologians of the Middle Ages recorded that men held the high intellect of angels, the reason of humankind, the intuition of animals, and the innate life force of the plant kingdom.

Wood Woman

SHE stands at the edge of the trees, as melancholy as the twilit woods she haunts. She holds much knowledge and knows many secrets, for the restless winds bring her messages from distant forests. The sound of each leaf's minute rustle is part of a great world arboreal eloquence. There is not a lone tree, bent low on the moor, that does not hear the murmur of rain forests on the other side of the earth.*

All forests are the domain of the faeries who make their homes in roots, branches, or right inside the heart of a tree—in which case their health and longevity are tied to that of the wood. In the vast woodlands of northern Europe you'll find many faery wood women, including the shy **skogsfru** of Denmark and the seductive **swor skogsfru** (wood wife) of Sweden. In Greece, the **dryads** (oak faeries), **melia** (ash faeries), and **caryatids** (nut faeries) are all types of **hamadryads** (wood faeries). In India, tree spirits called the **yakshi** protect the trees under their charge.

Wood women are fertility spirits, imbued with a sensuality as wild and mysterious as the moonlit groves of an ancient forest. They are famous for seducing humans, luring them deep into the woods. Afterward, the discarded lover will pine away for want of their touch. Sometimes **wood women** even marry humans, but usually this is not a success. These wood creatures are too wild and eventually flee back to their forests. As more and more ancient woodlands are destroyed by civilization, the wood faeries have been forced to retreat into the remaining forests and groves, zealously guarding their homes. Irreverent, unthinking human destruction creates fierce opposition in some wood faeries; while others, in sorrow at the loss of their homes, "die" back into the soil.

The **wood woman** represents a state of divine wildness and abandonment to natural rhythms, cycles, forces—an aspect of the **Goddess** (the personification of the life-giving forces of nature) in her primal, vegetative state. We feel her touch upon our lives not only in times of deep communion with nature, but also in moments of wordless rapture when we are dancing, singing, listening to music, making art, or making love. Look, she is still standing there at the edge of the wood, smiling slightly, drawing you deeper into the gloaming. Her hair is tangled with dried leaves and moss; her scent is of new green leaves and earth. Suddenly she is gone, and all that is left is the distant sound of her laughter. Do you weep for the joy of having seen her, or for the loss of her now that she's gone? Listen to the voice of the wind in the trees. It has a message for you.

Humans, too, have heard voices in the trees and learned to understand them. In the divinatory art of phyllomancy, the rustle of the wind in the trees serves an oracular function, answering questions and providing information about the future. The ancient **Druids used tree oracles, creating a tree alphabet to express the mystical connection between trees and knowledge. Greeks used laurel for prophecy at the **Delphic Oracle**.*

Fox Fire Faery

Fox Fire is the Irish name for this faery of the will-o'-the-wisp type (the elusive creatures who flicker into and out of vision, famed for leading travelers astray). Like the fox, this faery has a great deal of innate cunning—in the old sense of the word "cunning": wisdom or knowledge. His powers of awareness are acute, his judgment finely balanced, and he can size up any situation in the twinkling of a pixie's eye. **Fox Fire Faery** can be found between solid ground and deep waters—or else between two courses of action. He is helpful in all decision making.

Boon

The faery companion called **Boon** protects children from suffering bad dreams.
In Norwegian folklore, this guardian spirit, called the **fylgja**, is a creature who comes in dreams to
give advice or warning, often in animal form. These protective spirits stay with a man or woman from
birth to the end of their lives, and then pass on within the family to the next generation of children.

Little Nell

Like **Athene** (the Wise Virgin who sprang fully formed from the head of Zeus), **Little Nell** is a beautiful thought springing from the head of wisdom and experience. "Nothing is either good or bad, but thinking made it so," wrote Shakespeare. This faery, formed of pure thought, aids in the clarity of our thinking, preventing false projections and guarding against unthinking compulsions.

A Muryan

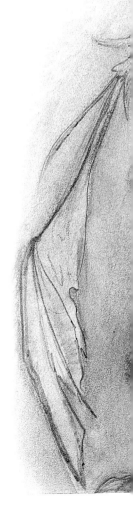

(right) The Cornish, in the far west of England, called their faeries **muryans**, or **ants**—because every time they shifted shape into rabbits or birds or other forms, they got progressively smaller in size, eventually becoming ant sized and then disappearing altogether. This particular **muryan** greets us from the distant past and speaks to us of longing as he connects us to our soul's home.

A Para, a Friendly Fertility Faery of Fluxility

A **para** is a domestic faery (Finnish in origin) who likes to appear in many forms, such as that of a strange cat, but prefers a froglike shape. This faery is famous in farmyards for increasing yields of milk and butter. She delights in working wherever there is a change of state: from grass to milk, from milk to cheese, from barley to beer, and (unfortunately) from food to fat. Having this faery for your companion may mean it will soon be diet time. She is also a fertility faery—but we must draw a veil of modesty over her antics in the bedroom.

Friendship Faeries

Faeries take particular joy in human children. It is said that
when a baby laughs, the faeries dance. Each child has a faery
companion, guarding him or her and watching over his or her
growth. Some children acknowledge these faeries and speak
openly of their "invisible friends" . . . but whether or not
children are aware of their particular faeries, the faeries
remain close by to secretly help them through the difficulties
of life.

   These faeries also help young children to make and
maintain friendships, and aid in all acts of mutual support.

The Faery Who Was Kissed by the Pixies

PERCHED upon her enchanted faery stool,* this faery shines with her own inner light while surrounded by saucy **pixies** and other tricksy creatures. She laughs with the joy that a **pixie** kiss brings. The **pixies** say there cannot be too much kissing! A faery kiss is a blessing indeed.

Some mushrooms are called toadstools, but I've never seen a toad sitting on one. I've often seen faeries perched on them, though, for toadstools and other fungi have always been linked to Faeryland. Toadstools emerge where the faeries have danced and are the preferred food of Welsh faeries. Having a plantlike structure but no chlorophyll, and an animal-like digestive system, toadstools and fungi are often referred to as the "third kingdom"—a true faery phenomenon.

People have always felt ambivalent toward these strange, mysterious forms pungent with life (in the form of food) and death (in the form of poison). Fungi are part of a vast system that includes yeasts and molds, agents of decay and disease—yet also a vital part of bread, intoxicant brews, and antibiotics. To indigenous peoples of Mexico and South America, certain mushrooms, called "God's flesh," provide gateways to other worlds. Siberian shamans use the fly agaric (the definitive faery toadstool) as a psychoactive drug to open psychic gateways, just as Celtic shamans once used Dartmoor's "magic mushrooms" in their rituals.

The fruiting body of the toadstool is but a brief, focused manifestation of a vast hidden underground system of fine filaments (called mycelia) all interconnected and penetrating large areas of soil. The true life of the fungi is not seen above but hidden below, underground. Fungi help decompose and transform worn-out material, moving it along the cycle of life, and thus, in faery lore, are a symbol of regeneration.

As many old folktales will tell you, where there are toadstools there are sure to be faeries. The next time you find one, listen for the laughter of a faery who may have just been kissed.

A Collective of Pixies

These faeries of the **pixie** type lurk at the very edges of consciousness, flickering and flittering, groping for light. They are not individuals, but rather have a group soul and a collective mind. Just as a single pixel on a computer screen requires many other pixels to form a whole picture, each **pixie** in this collective is just one fragment making up a whole thought. Knowing **pixies**, it's probably a very short thought!

King of the Pixies

(overleaf) Although **pixies** are famous for leading travelers astray with their flickering faery lights, this magnificent **phosphorescent pouk** is the flash of light, of insight, that leads you *away* from danger. He gives you that sudden spark of intuition warning of danger: Don't go down that street, don't trust that person, don't sign that contract, don't accept that proposal. He warns us not to go on blindly, urging us to be awake and aware, and to choose our way with care.

A Hedgerow Pixie

(overleaf) In mischievous moods, this **hedgerow pixie** might push bramble thorns into your path. Yet when you are firmly entangled, if you listen carefully to him, he will whisper the wisdom of nature and the ancient healing properties of plants. This faery is the particular friend of herbalists and homeopaths.

A Positive Pixie

(left) This **pixie** is very helpful to have around, especially when you are serving spaghetti or unraveling a knotty problem.

A COLLECTIVE OF PIXIES

KING OF THE PIXIES

A HEDGEROW PIXIE

Pixies

PIXIES are the exuberant natural gymnasts of Faeryland, leaping through the air like salmon through a stream. Although they are creatures of air and earth, they love water particularly. They adore damp places and wet climates—which is why they are found in abundance here in our rain-soaked landscape of Dartmoor, where they delight in leading travelers crossing the moor into bogs and mires. To be "**pixy** led" is to be enchanted into a trancelike state ("mazed," as they say here on Dartmoor), lost, and completely disoriented. Many of our local place-names testify to a haunting by mischievous **pixies**: Pixies Holt, Pixies Cave, Pixies Cleave, Pixies Parlour, to name but a few. "There's piskies up to Dartmoor," farmers insist in the old dialect, and "t'idden gude yu sez there bain't!"

John Fitz, who lived across the moor in Tavistock in the sixteenth century, fell under a **pixie** spell and was **pixy** led for many weary hours until he found a spring to refresh his body and clear his mind. He later placed a stone at the spring as an aid to other travelers, and there it stands to this very day as protection against the **pixies'** pranks. A woman from the same town claimed that her baby sister had once been stolen by local **pixies** and a faery changeling left in the infant's place. The woman cared for the changeling so well that the pixies returned her own child, safe and sound and happy after its sojourn in Faeryland.

In another local incident, the outcome was not so happy. One winter eve a small voice was heard in the twilight out upon the moor, calling the name of a young farm lad: "Jan Coo, Jan Coo, Jan Coo . . ." Each night the voice sounded closer and closer, and finally Jan could resist no longer. He wandered out into the darkness and was never seen again.

Many accounts can be found of **pixies** leaving gifts or helping out at night with household and farmyard chores—yet it cannot be denied that they are happiest being naughty. They like to steal horses, tangling their manes, knotting their tails, riding them to exhaustion. Similarly, they delight in tangling girls' hair, pinching their arms, and keeping them from sleep. They love to dance in rising dough, flattening it with their tiny feet, and to curdle cheese, and to sour cream or wine or kegs of beer. Most of all they like to blow out lamps and kiss pretty lasses under cover of darkness.

When **pixies** are inclined to be helpful, one must remember to thank them with bowls of cream or beer left by the hearth. A gift of clothes, though kindly meant, will generally give the **pixies** offense. A Cornish farmer was grateful to a hardworking **pixie** who thrashed his corn by night, and so the farmwife made the naked creature a fine suit of clothes. Greatly offended, the **pixie** cried, "Pisky fine and pisky gay, now pisky will fly away!" and never was seen again. What the farmer did not realize was that nakedness, in the faery realm, is considered a highly honorable state. Naked, we are stripped of all pretensions, open to the most subtle forces of spirit and nature. The faeries will always resist attempts to impose human rules and mores on them. They ask that we take them as they are—and thus a gift of clothes (unless specifically requested) can be misconstrued as a crude attempt to bind or control them. Because of their great love of water, a water basin left by the fire at night is a better way to please a **pixie**. High-diving frolics in rivers and pools are also known to make them happy. When **pixies** have been thus entertained, they sometimes leave a coin for reward— but this must be kept strictly secret or they will never be so generous again.

Observing the agile antics of **pixies** reminds us all to be agile ourselves, flexible in our approach to life and its daily problems. A rigid branch will break in a storm, but the flexible reeds and grasses bend and then quickly straighten again. The **pixies** and other plantlike faeries bend in the face of adversity, bend and twist and do not break. They swim in the wild wind of a storm, moving *with* and not *against* the flow, riding the powerful currents of possibility and change.

The Wise Fool of Faery

(*opposite*) Considered by some to be one of the most important figures in Faeryland, the **Wise Fool** turns our rigid perceptions upside down. He shows us that opposites are each contained in the other: that there is light in darkness, growth in decay, good in bad and vice versa. He is the sacred **Fool** of the tarot card deck, and the clever clown of Trickster myths. He reminds us that there is nonsense in dogma, and truth or sense in nonsense.

A Diet Hob

Although he traditionally lives in food cupboards, the modern hob has also been known to take up residence in refrigerators. He's the one who urges you to eat things you don't need, like chocolate candy bars and entire pints of ice cream. He is especially associated with packs of cookies, urging you to open the wrapping in order to eat just one . . . and then, of course, to keep on going. This **hob** is the faery who destroys all good intentions when you're trying to diet.

Oak Men

"Faery folks live in old oaks," states a rhyme from the West Country lore of England. These creatures are guardians of ancient oaks, such as those to be found near my home on Dartmoor. They tempt passersby with toadstools enchanted to resemble delicious morsels of food. In the gloaming, you can hear them murmur: "As above, so below."

Topsy-Turvies

(*overleaf*) **Robert Kirk**, writing of the faery faith in the Highlands of Scotland, reported that our summer is their winter, our day is their night, and that faeries are always outside of our scale of time. Faeryland is a reverse image of the human world—when our fruits decay, theirs ripen, and faery lambs bleat in November.

Faeryland is a topsy-turvy world, full of mirror reversals and paradox. The largest of faery lands can be contained within the smallest of things, and the wisest of faery minds within the most insignificant of creatures. In the faery realms, it is the **Fool** who is wisest of all—for foolishness is wisdom revisited, wisdom in reverse. Faery has often been represented as a world upside down in relation to ours, not only in its physical nature but in the thought processes of its denizens. Through this topsy-turvy worldview of the faeries we are prompted to look at our own lives from a new, contrary perspective, questioning our preconceived notions and received wisdom.

Street Corner Lurker

This capricious creature decides which side of a piece of buttered toast ends up facedown when it is dropped.

Buttered Toast Faery

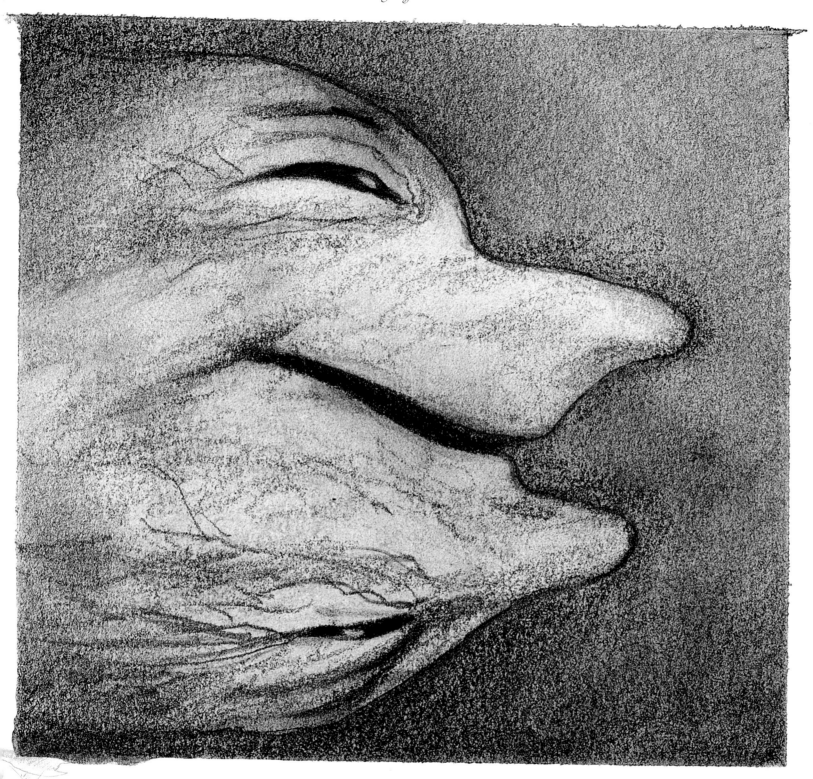

When I've made a wrong turn, or wrong choice, or bad business decision, or put on an unfortunate choice of clothes, this faery has been at my side.

The Wrong-Decision Faery

Treasure Guardian

(opposite) Many faeries guard hidden treasures, the Irish leprechauns being the best known of them. Secret crocks of gold have been the lure for many seeking Faeryland. But those who succeed in winning or stealing the faeries' wealth often find to their dismay that faery gold soon transforms back into leaves with a golden hue (back into nature herself).

These treasure seekers do not understand that true faery treasure is not the gold of the physical world, but the gold of the spirit.

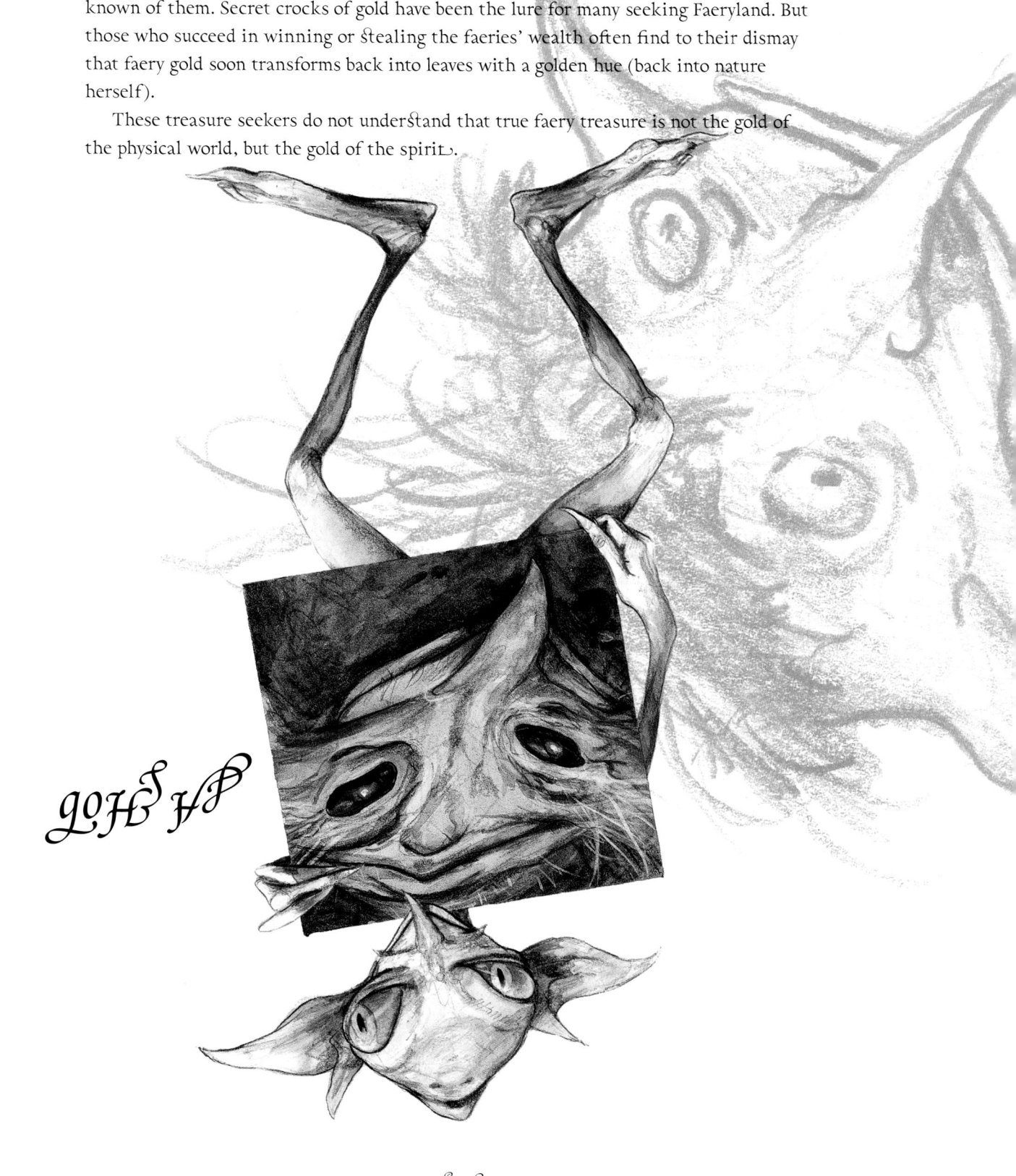

Bwbach, or Boobach

This household faery lives in Wales but has been known to travel. **Bwbach** is good natured but quite mischievous: he pulls faces, makes dogs howl, frightens babies, and lifts old ladies' skirts up. His very favorite prank is to whisk people through the air. He is also known to have a strong aversion to those who abstain from strong drink.

Little Blighter

Gardeners and farmers know this faery all too well. He causes blights, rots, spots, rusts, mildews, molds, scabs, and wilts on fruits and vegetables.

A Boggart

A wayward brownielike creature who often has a sharp, pointed nose, he's the perpetrator of little problems affecting the things around us. He doesn't think his tinkerings matter, and yet they render objects useless. He is the cause behind scratches on records and CDs, chips in glasses, punctures in tires, and bursting balloons.

The Allergy Faery

This faery causes a sense of prickliness against the world and, through misplaced sensitivity, produces various allergies.

Bogle

(opposite) This **bogle** causes eye problems, especially squints and lazy eyes—eyes that look in and out. If pleased, however, he gives the gift of clear sight in the inner as well as the outer world—"in-sight." With this gift we can see the faeries.

Squinter

Originating on the Isle of Man, **Squinters** (also known as **Sleigh Beggys**) are famous for their naked appearance. They live underground, dislike artificial light, and hate the taste of salt. The sight of ashes will throw these faeries into a terrible temper. On the other hand, snow makes them very happy.

One further note: Although no one knows why, it is extremely advisable never, ever to mention a **Squinter**'s feet. As anyone who has ever met a **Squinter** knows to his cost, it provokes an unseemly, ill-tempered, and foul-mouthed display.

The Faery Pisser

After November Eve (Halloween), the country people of Dartmoor declare that blackberries and sloes are not fit to eat, for the "faeries piss on them." This faery is related to the mischievous Irish **pooka**, who stamps on the last blackberries of the season.

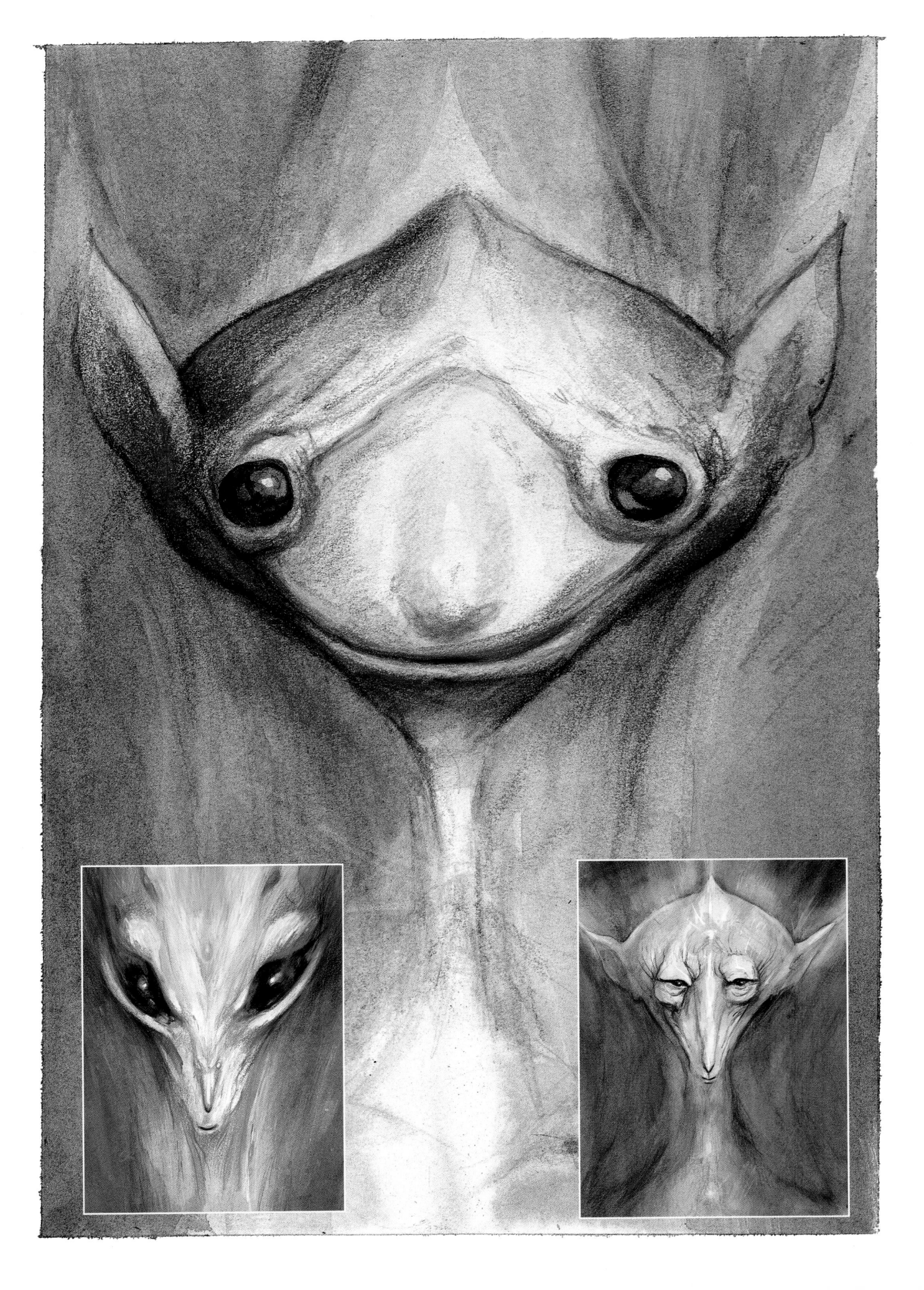

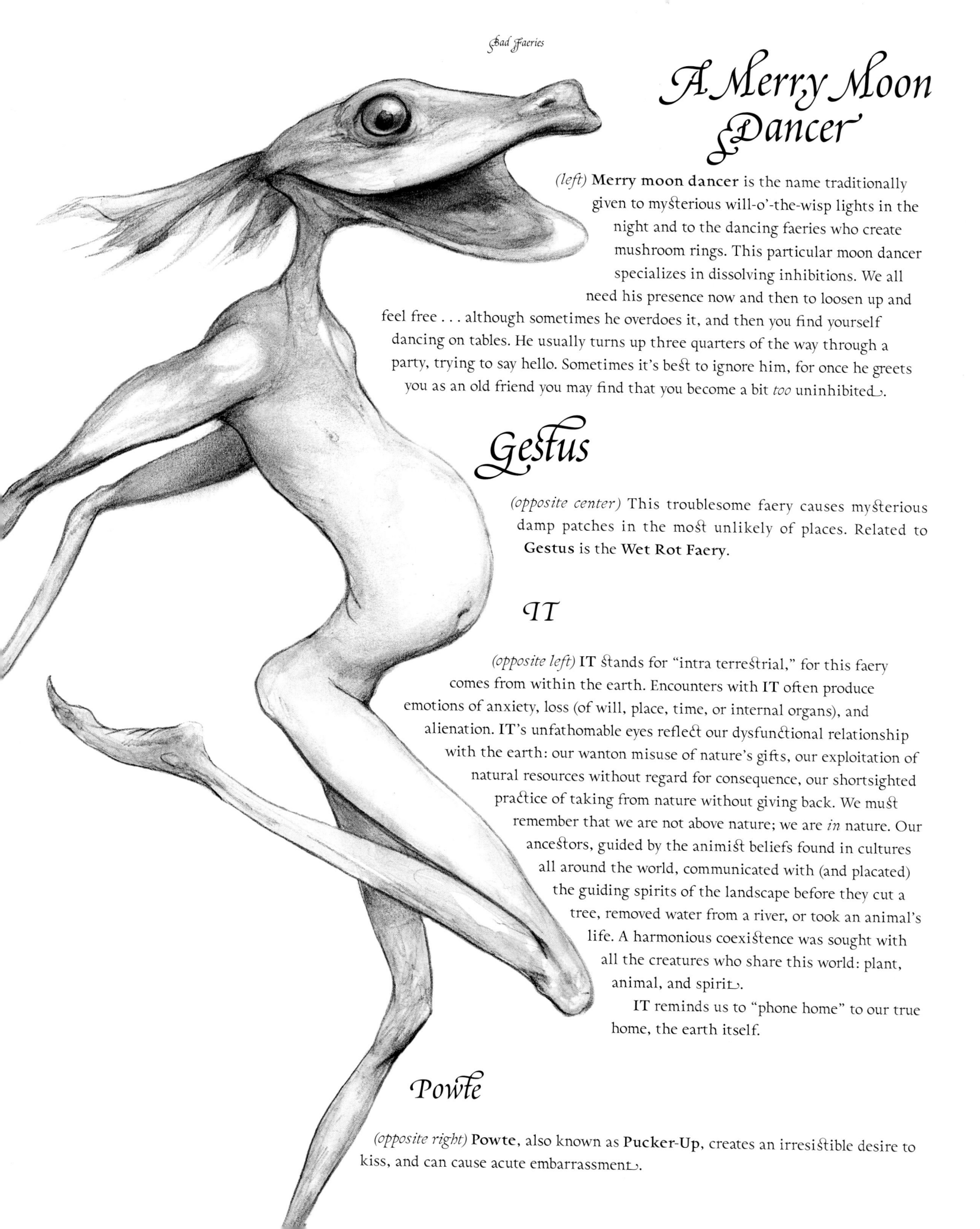

A Merry Moon Dancer

(left) **Merry moon dancer** is the name traditionally given to mysterious will-o'-the-wisp lights in the night and to the dancing faeries who create mushroom rings. This particular moon dancer specializes in dissolving inhibitions. We all need his presence now and then to loosen up and feel free . . . although sometimes he overdoes it, and then you find yourself dancing on tables. He usually turns up three quarters of the way through a party, trying to say hello. Sometimes it's best to ignore him, for once he greets you as an old friend you may find that you become a bit *too* uninhibited.

Gestus

(opposite center) This troublesome faery causes mysterious damp patches in the most unlikely of places. Related to **Gestus** is the **Wet Rot Faery**.

IT

(opposite left) **IT** stands for "intra terrestrial," for this faery comes from within the earth. Encounters with **IT** often produce emotions of anxiety, loss (of will, place, time, or internal organs), and alienation. **IT**'s unfathomable eyes reflect our dysfunctional relationship with the earth: our wanton misuse of nature's gifts, our exploitation of natural resources without regard for consequence, our shortsighted practice of taking from nature without giving back. We must remember that we are not above nature; we are *in* nature. Our ancestors, guided by the animist beliefs found in cultures all around the world, communicated with (and placated) the guiding spirits of the landscape before they cut a tree, removed water from a river, or took an animal's life. A harmonious coexistence was sought with all the creatures who share this world: plant, animal, and spirit.

IT reminds us to "phone home" to our true home, the earth itself.

Powte

(opposite right) **Powte**, also known as **Pucker-Up**, creates an irresistible desire to kiss, and can cause acute embarrassment.

Pot Pixie

Often associated with the rather strange and lurid *Boletus erythropus*, this annoying faery is frequently found in my kitchen, where it causes milk and soup (particularly mushroom soup) to boil over and stews to erupt from under pan lids, creating a dreadful mess. The Scots are plagued by a **pot pixie** that plays havoc with their porridge. The old saying "A watched pot never boils" derives from the antics of the **pot pixies**. Take your eyes off the pot for a moment, and *whoosh*—pixilated porridge all over the stove!

The Crumb Faery

This creature puts crumbs in the bed in delicate patterns that have great meaning to the faeries.

An Oddly Familiar Gnome

This oddly familiar gnome is sometimes helpful, but usually not—for although he means well, he appears rather unfocused and seldom sober. He blunders into situations, causing upsets and misunderstandings. He claims to be the companion of the **Wise Fool** . . . but this I doubt.

The Out-of-the-Blue Faery

He wakes you in the night with a sudden realization: you forgot to mail a letter, pay a bill, switch off an iron, buy an anniversary gift . . .

Morgana le Fay

MORGANA is one of the greatest of all faery queens. She is skilled in necromancy and the ancient art of shape shifting, able to be whatever she desires. She soars through the night on raven's wings, landing silently in your dreams to work her dark enchantments. Well versed in star craft and arcane healing powers (with knowledge gleaned from **Merlin** himself), she is the mistress of the mystical arts of sexuality and high magic.

Hers is a complex nature, neither totally beneficent nor totally malign. Her faults are anger, resentment, and, true to faery nature, using her cunning arts against those who offend her. Yet although she schemes against **King Arthur** (her half brother), it is on her lap that he rests his dying head as she and two other dark queens sail him to Avalon to be healed. It is her necessary role to be found at the crux of the drama in our lives, working toward wisdom and healing in dramatic, difficult times. She guides in moments of forceful emotions such as anger, bitterness, resentment, and sexual jealousy. The disturbing influence of this dark queen can lead to profound change.

The three powerful days at the dark of the moon are this faery's special time—when all processes are internalized and concealed. It is then that Morgana comes to us to reveal the mystical starlight, the bright points of faery consciousness, which permeates all of matter. Morgana is an enchantress who works her magic at the deepest levels—in the dark, secret, hidden places of our minds. She initiates us into mystic realms of creative imagination where all that is not yet manifest begins the journey into light and form.

A Disruptive Bogle

A particularly disruptive **bogle** creating confusion, mix-ups, crossed lines, and misunderstandings. I think he has taken up residence in my house. His mischief causes e-mails to be sent to the wrong addresses, faxes to arrive garbled or half printed, and mobile phones to go down. In general, he causes havoc in all communications.

ℒeanan Sidhe

This beguiling creature is the Irish faery mistress, or faery muse, who inspires artists, poets, and musicians. Her enchantments stimulate creativity until it burns with a bright, fierce flame. The sheer intensity of this vision will eventually leave the artist hollow eyed and worn, his gift in ashes. Artists visited by the **Leanan Sidhe** are said to be touched by genius but often die young.

In other moods, she is the **Dark Seductress** known as **Lhiannan Shee** on the Isle of Man. She seduces her victim, draws out his spirit, and leaves him as a ruined husk in body and soul. She is the **skogsfru** of Scandinavia, a forest faery with a fatal touch; and the **Bonga Maiden** of India, a capricious nature spirit who entices and even marries human men. She is the beautiful **Deer Maiden** of the Lakota and other Native American tribes, who lures men into the woods to their doom—yet also inspires artists (and occasionally drives them mad). But she is perhaps best known as the faery so evocatively portrayed in Keats's poem "La Belle Dame sans Merci": the seductive creature who leaves the knight haggard, alone, and "palely loitering."

A Small Pan, or a Slight Panic

This irresistible child of the great **Pan** himself hides in secret nooks and crannies, ready to leap out in pursuit of the unwary (especially pretty young girls and attractive goats). His presence causes minor pandemonium and slight panic, so be cautious of things that pop out suddenly from hidden places.

Hinkey-Punk

(left) Daytime mists that shroud the land are common on the hills of Dartmoor, and it's easy to become lost and disoriented. Equally, dark moonless nights are no friend to the unfortunate traveler. Flickering will-o'-the-wisp lights appear, seeming to offer safe guidance . . . but don't follow them. They are actually the work of the **hinkey-punk**, a faery who delights in luring the unwary to their death at the bottom of treacherous bogs, precipitous rocks, and turbulent rivers.

The eerie lights of a village churchyard at midnight are also to be avoided, for here the **hinkey-punk** meets the souls of the dead and guides them on their journey. These lights, moving in long processions from churchyards up to the Moorland Way, are known as corpse candles. Be careful, lest your own soul's light be compelled to joint that lambent line.

The Ear Poker

(right) This faery's delight is to poke her faery finger into one of your ears while jabbering into the other. Faery talk is often backward, and very shrill or birdlike. This naturally causes confusion in humans. Sudden silences, loss of connection, and disorientation are sure signs that the ear poker is nearby.

Spunkies

(left) **Spunkies**, closely related to **hinkey-punks**, are malicious faeries who lead us into danger. Haunting dark or misty landscapes with their flickering faery lights, they cruelly lead people astray . . . to the sound of spunky laughter. Out at sea, these lights of hollow hope have led to shipwrecks and the death of many sailors. Beware of **spunkies** and the bright false promises they hold out to you.

The Credit Card Faery

(top) This bad faery causes confusion in credit card transactions. It lurks in cash dispensers, spits out your card, and keeps your money. Its adverse influence creates chaos on the magnetic strip, and then your card ceases to function—or it functions too well, causing funds to flow to mysterious recipients.

Bright Borrower Faery

(opposite left) One of the many groups of light-fingered thieves of Faeryland, these crafty little fellows cannot keep their fingers off anything. Like jackdaws, they are irresistibly attracted to all shiny objects, from diamond rings to candy wrappers, and steal them away to hide in various secret faery places. They say that they are just borrowing these objects, but faeries are very bad timekeepers. By the time they remember to return the things they've taken (usually many years later), they've forgotten where they hid them. Faeries have been known to discover their own hoards and, having forgotten they were theirs, to borrow their own borrowings!

Bright Borrowers lead lives of quiet contentment—although squabbles over stolen goods sometimes occur. They greatly enjoy the inconvenience they cause, delighting in frantic human searches. Human curses give these faeries particular merriment.

Matchless Faery

He makes matches damp, extinguishes that last vital match, and is a secret guzzler of lighter fluid. He has a general dampening, depressing effect on the atmosphere of rooms, parties, and relationships.

Mr. Despair & Mr. Despondency

When these two come knocking at my door, I don't let them in! Their presence creates negative thoughts, their baleful gaze of self-pity penetrates the miasmic gloom around them. I keep the door firmly shut until I hear their shuffling footsteps fade, knowing that soon a brighter faery will come to call.

The Glanconer

FOLKTALES abound of elfin seductresses who lure men into the woods and to their doom. Less well known but just as lethal is the masculine faery seducer.

In Ireland, he is known as the **Glanconer**, or **Love Talker**. His amorous cousins around the world include England's deadly **Reynardine**, the **fox daemons** of China and Japan, the lusty **elk men** of Dakota myth, certain **dark-eyed jinns** of Arabia, and the amorous, treacherous **elfin knight** of Scottish balladry.

The **Glanconer**'s eyes are black as sloes and his words are sweeter than honey. He walks the woods by twilight, prowling for women to charm and kiss. Beware. Dealing with the **Love Talker** involves a risk—an elemental risk. It might be an exhilarating experience treasured for the rest of your life—or you might pine away when the faery's gone and no other man's touch can equal his. The **Glanconer**, like sweet-talking human lover boys, takes you for a walk on the wild side of Faery. It could be the making of you . . . or lead to pain and despair.

One of the Glanconer's Gang

(below left) This amoral faery is one of the **Glanconer**'s companions. Use extreme caution when dealing with this creature and the rest of his lot. They can create, in humans, emotions of happiness so intense they hurt. In fact, pain is their joy. They break hearts and give very nasty bites.

The Abductor

(below right) This furtive faery steals away children, who are never to be seen again.

The Foot Fungus Faery

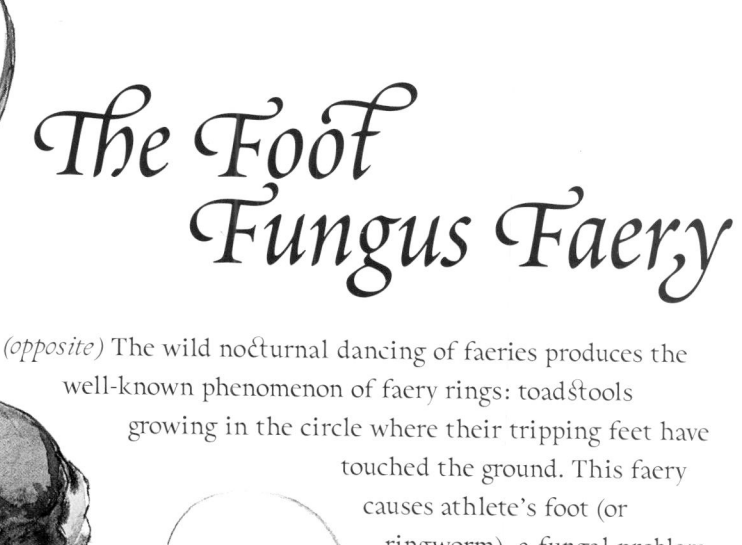

(*opposite*) The wild nocturnal dancing of faeries produces the well-known phenomenon of faery rings: toadstools growing in the circle where their tripping feet have touched the ground. This faery causes athlete's foot (or ringworm), a fungal problem of the skin in ring-shaped patches. It is a fungal faery ring, personalized and in miniature. One book of remedies recommends that we "go artistic" and wear sandals without socks—in other words, give freedom to our feet; let them be less constricted and more creative. Our feet connect us to the ground and give firm footing to bright ideas and flights of fancy. Sometimes we need to earth our dreams in order to bring them to fruition.

The **foot fungus faery**, like the mushroom he sits on, has materialized overnight. He is an idea just coming into form. His wings are still damp and crumpled, not yet fully extended. He sits, making the decision whether to sit or stand or fly away—whichever might be the best foot forward. This faery can slow you down or help you develop a surefooted future.*

The Pen Stealer

This exasperating faery steals pens and other small objects from schoolbags.

*I suspect this creature moonlights as the faery sock stealer.

GUARDIAN OF THE BLACKTHORN BUSH

MELSH DICK

A FEE LION

A Fee Lion

THE **Fee Lion** is not one of the larger species of faery. Because of its diminutive size, it is commonly known as a **Slight Accusation**, or else an **Accusation of Slight**. Here we see the look that all cat owners know so well: "You *know* I have my dinner at five o'clock." (Bearing in mind that cats have always been witches' favorite familiars, perhaps another name for the **Fee Lion** should be **That Old Familiar Feeling**.)

This faery is the creator of small disturbances, such as faint scratchings in the early hours or mysterious midnight mewings. Traditionally he is heard inside cupboards and bedrooms—always on the other side of doors. This is the faery to blame when your keys are left inside a locked car or hotel room. He is a creature who needs a lot of attention, for his feelings are easily ruffled. But if you make the effort to get him on your side he will act in your best interest, and then you will always be in the right place at the right time.

The **Fee Lion** is also the voice that reminds you to do the little things that matter to someone other than yourself: feed the dog, clean the hamster's cage, write a thank-you note, spend more time with Great-aunt Martha. He is the faery of things that scratch and mew inside your head as you're falling asleep, those little "You know you should" voices that always have a slightly accusing tone. Try doing what he asks, and you'll find you have fewer disturbances from this faery.

Melsh Dick

(*overleaf*) **Melsh Dick** is the Yorkshire faery who protects unripe nuts. Nuts of all kinds are dear to the faeries, and the act of nutting often draws them to you. A female gathering nuts in a wood is in particular danger of faery attention of an amorous nature.

Guardian of the Blackthorn Bush

(*overleaf*) The blackthorn is one of the most sacred plants of Faery. Its white blossoms herald the spring and are used in May Day celebrations. But the faeries jealously guard the treasure of blackthorn fruits (sloes), which have a beautiful, magical bloom that disappears when picked. If you've ever attempted to pick faery fruit and to take what is not yours, you already know that the nails and teeth of faeries are painfully sharp!

A Frisky Faery

(above) This faery frequents steps, stiles, and slopes, causing a certain slipperiness that makes us lose our footing. From the level ground, flat on our backs, we may gain a new perspective.

Bad Hair Day Faery

(below) Folklore tells us that faeries take a wicked pleasure in tangling hair—particularly in the country, where they love to knot the manes and tails of horses and cattle. For city faeries, it is human hair that they find to be irresistible. Little faery fingers are busy in the night . . . and we wake to another bad hair day.

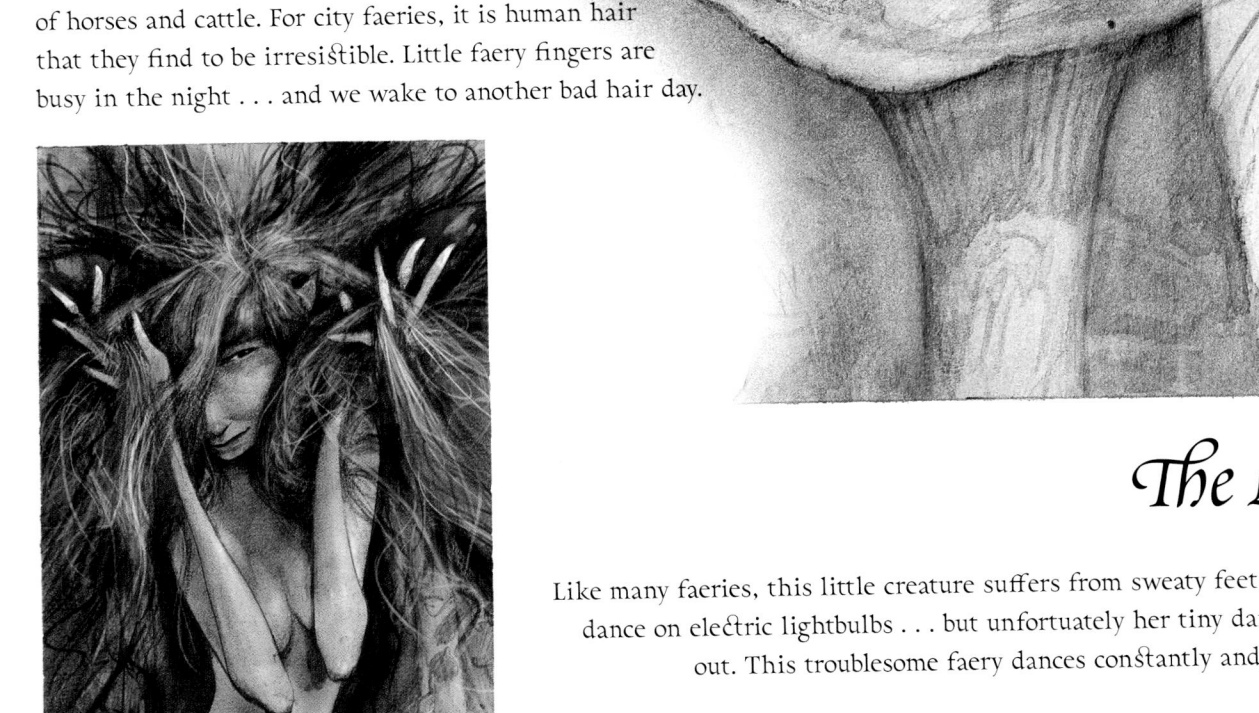

The Light Dancer

Like many faeries, this little creature suffers from sweaty feet. Attracted to light, she loves to dance on electric lightbulbs . . . but unfortuately her tiny damp feet always make them blow out. This troublesome faery dances constantly and rampantly through my house.

Hobthrust

Hobthrust is a particularly mischievous household faery, infuriatingly fond of pulling down zippers, tucking skirts up at the back, putting runs in stockings, loosening buttons, and untying shoelaces. Despite this interest in our clothes, **Hobthrust** does not wear any himself. He was once kindly offered a set of clothes and was mortally offended. "Ha!" he cried, "a cloack and a hood, hob'll never do mair good!" and he promptly vanished.

A Grinling

Just when you think nothing more can go wrong, a **grinling** appears.

A Frid

Frids are faeries who live in or under rocks and take food crumbs left on the ground. They are partial to spilled milk, over which they have never been known to cry. **Frids** get very angry over casual destruction of nature by humans. They trip up those who are careless, or who care less about the earth. These days, these formerly solitary creatures can be found more and more in urban settings, taking a keen interest in the state of roads and pavements.

Lilu

Crouching on the edge of reason, just beyond rationality, this faery is the provocateur of restless nights and erotic dreams. She is the one who ensnares us with compulsions, fixations, feverish imaginings. Yet within the dark tangle of images she weaves are the glittering threads of our own healing—for even as she conjures our compulsions she holds out the ability to release their grip, enabling us to confront and let go of all that we no longer need.

Rarr

One of these faeries used to whiz through my son's bedroom when he was very young, and often he'd come into our bed complaining that **Rarrs** and the **Pink Boys** were keeping him awake. We discovered that the **Pink Boys** were naughty faeries who loved to pull ridiculous faces and to leap out suddenly at our son, making him cry. They thought that this was the best game ever, until we had a talk with them. I asked them to please go back to their home in the corner of our garden, where they have remained and been remarkably well behaved ever since.

We never did find out who or what the **Rarr** was. It disappeared about this time and never returned.

The Wild Crouch, or the Reckless Wrecker

He crouches on the front of your car and tells you to go faster: You can do it. There's enough room. Go on . . . pass now. Squeeze through; you can do it. Faster, faster, faster'.

But listen to him at your peril, for he is immortal and you are not.

This faery is quick and slippery and you must always keep him in your sight. He jumps like a grasshopper out of your view, only to reappear alarmingly when you least expect him. The **Wild Crouch** is the dark cousin of Trickster figures around the world: **Loki** in Norse mythology, **Uncle Tompa** in Tibetan folklore, **Anansi the Spider** in Africa, and **Coyote** in Native American tales, all of whom have reckless, dangerous pranks in their bag of tricks. (The **Crouch**'s female counterpart is **Ate**, the goddess of mischief from early Greek mythology, who incites men to crime and sows discord among the gods.) The green fire of envy and jealousy drives this faery's destructive mischief making. If he lands on your head you may find yourself acting recklessly, taking unusually foolish risks, or succumbing to excesses of vice and gambling.

An Insomnia Faery

A highly intrusive faery who is tiresome in the night.

The Rust Spot Faery

YESTERDAY this faery told me she was a slight madness engendered by eating too much bacon . . . but I don't believe everything a faery says. Today she states that she is the one who maintains correct levels of iron in the blood. Her work is in the liver, recycling iron. If this faery becomes vague and inattentive, anemia can result.

In this faery form, we see female energy moving into balance with the male. Iron* represents stasis; it is inflexible and masculine. The intransigence of iron is transformed, when it rusts, by the feminine aspects of water and oxygen, the very essence of life. Rust, then, is formed of the cold reason of iron transformed into red oxide; the color represents passion, life renewal, and the blood of the earth. Shamans used body paint made of red oxide in many mystical rites, and in the ancient world it was used for ritual decoration of corpses and bones. Water of a rusty color was deemed to have magical properties—such as the famous healing waters of Holy Chalice Well in Glastonbury, England.

This rusty faery interacts with us on many different levels, concerned particularly with bodily health, decay, and regeneration. But you might know her best in one of her more annoying guises: as the cause of that first rust spot on a shiny new chrome surface.

A Tongue Tangler *(left)*

A note on rust: Faeries have their origin in the pretechnological past. Classical writers refer to a Silver Age, a time when man's mind moved more easily in intuitive and creative modes. Silver is a faery metal, influenced by the moon and Mercury, that enhances communication and connection. After the Age of Silver was the Age of Iron, which brought us reason, ambition, and warfare; thus it is no wonder that the faeries' relationship with iron is ambivalent. Many faeries are frightened by iron—a nail or knife or open scissors are traditionally used to keep faeries away. Other faeries, the borrowing faeries, are just the opposite; they find anything iron irresistible (especially kettles and cauldrons) and delight in stealing it. Being faeries, they get overexcited and will carry off almost anything—as you discover when you try to find that whatchamacallit that was going to be so useful . . . and you know you put it down right here . . . and now it's gone . . . it just walked away.

Actually, it's in a faery nest in a glittering collection of "lost" objects.

Anxious Annie

THIS anxious, fretful, high-strung creature stands on my chest wringing her hands or sits on my shoulder nibbling my ear, making me more and more worried, more and more convinced of impending disaster. When I find myself paralyzed by nerves, or pacing the floor at 2 A.M. imagining every little thing that might go wrong, when I'm fretting and fussing and feeling like a fool, **Anxious Annie** is around. There's no getting rid of her with force; she's timid but tenacious. The only defense is to get her laughing, at which point she becomes rather endearing.

Gurney the Face Puller

He sours milk—and relationships.

The Yellow Blurker

(*opposite*) You may know him as the **Grubling Gob**, or the **Vile Blurker**, or even as the **Magpie of Hades**. His color is a bilious yellow, not the clear gold of his brother, the **Retriever**. Whether he's stealing your hopes or your golf balls, he spirits them away forever, never to be found again. He carries your dreams off with his toes, holding them as far from himself as possible. And then he says slyly: "It wasn't me. Look, my hands are empty."

Nothing is safe from this devious, negative creature. When that important letter is lost in the mail, when you inexplicably forget to do something vital, when your best intentions go awry . . . this is the faery at work.

The Compulsive Faery

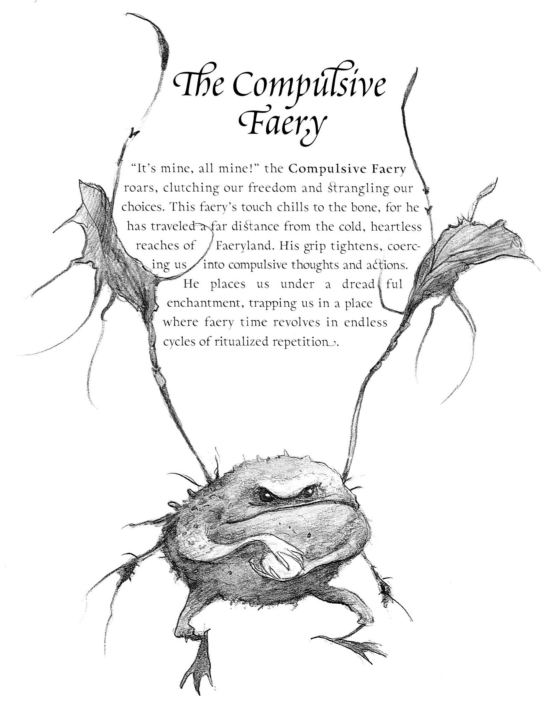

"It's mine, all mine!" the **Compulsive Faery** roars, clutching our freedom and strangling our choices. This faery's touch chills to the bone, for he has traveled a far distance from the cold, heartless reaches of Faeryland. His grip tightens, coercing us into compulsive thoughts and actions. He places us under a dreadful enchantment, trapping us in a place where faery time revolves in endless cycles of ritualized repetition.

A Slippery Faery

All faeries are elusive (and illusive) creatures. This faery is particularly slippery, making objects slip out of your fingers and smash against the floor. She haunts kitchens, and glassware shops, and posh ceramics galleries. She also contrives slips of the tongue: when you are under her influence, the wrong word just slips right out of your mouth. Her specialty is the Freudian slip, which reveals too much about yourself.

An Obscure Faery

As the faery of green molds and algae, she is especially fond of the inside of fish tanks. While generally benign in nature, this creature can become quite dangerous if she stays around too long.

Just as algae slowly cover glass, this faery slowly obscures our vision, making it difficult to see ourselves or the world with true clarity. Her lingering touch can cloud our thoughts with ignorance and prejudice. Clear away her influence, and the vision of truth shines through once more.

Melancholic Faery

When humans glimpse the faery realm, these visions are often accompanied by a feeling of being out of time. In one sense, Faery is a land of the past, where the spirit world and the human world once worked in closer harmony. In the faeries' presence, we experience a nostalgic yearning for that time . . . and for all lost hopes and all lost dreams, all that once was or might have been (and may someday be again). Promises we haven't kept come back to haunt us in this faery's eyes.

The Faery of Dark Despair

She throws her spell of introspective darkness, and you sink deeper into the shadows of despondency. Her enchantment may last for just a few hours . . . or for many years. Yet the hue of her wings reminds us that there is always hope in the midst of hopelessness.

The Fluff Faery

(below) You may have glimpsed this fuzzy fellow out of the corner of your eye. Fluff is his favorite substance. He lives under a bed, down the back of a sofa, or inside a vacuum cleaner (his idea of faery heaven). He doesn't mean to cause harm, but he just can't help getting fluff on new CDs or sticky candy. Hair in the soap is evidence that he's been in the bathroom. He's the one who puts specks on camera lenses, creating hazy horizons; he's been known to cause furred-up pipes and thus slow down the flow of things. This little creature is prone to depression, and sitting near him can engender woolly thinking. Make friends with him to prevent his mischief and regain clarity.

A Small Pang of Regret

(above) I found this faery at the place in our garden where the Chinese rhubarb plant had been wantonly knocked to the ground. He couldn't talk, but he communicated by shaking and nodding his head. Because of this, it took me a long while to discover just who he was: the memory of the form of the plant before it had been vandalized. He held the imprint of what the plant had been before, a necessary pattern for what it would be in the future. Although as a faery of regret he can be sad, painful, or disturbing, without him the plant would have no foundation for new growth in the year to come. Faeries of this type, giving form to all manner of regrets and unresolved memories, often hide in the muscles and the joints, and can— when they get stuck there—cause painful physical problems. A faery's natural state is movement; faeries are never meant to be static. When this **Pang of Regret** was allowed to be free again, his purpose acknowledged, he swam through the air like a fish, with beautiful undulating movements. This faery is the facilitator who links the future with the past.

The Gloominous Doom

(left) Let me introduce an old friend of mine. In the dark depths of depression, the **Gloominous Doom** despairs and moans, "I can't do it," slump shouldered, his wings leaking drips of light. He holds the globe of clear thinking unexamined behind him. The globe contains all his lost hopes, turned heavy with his pessimism. "It's too late now," he sighs wearily. "It's all behind me now."

Ask him to toss that hope forward, where it becomes a perfect sphere. Step into it, protected and secure in the light of clarity—and the shuffling step of the **Gloominous Doom** becomes the dance of the **Luminous Loon**.

Indi, the Indecision Faery

(right) While one expects to find a faery strolling down an English country lane, this faery might be found in an American bowling lane instead. In fact, this troublesome creature can pop up anywhere: he's the one that won't let you make up your mind, perpetually weighing the pros and cons. Is it a left-handed *should* or a right-handed *shouldn't*? Or maybe it's the other way around. Ask him to let the energy go, and he just may bowl you over with a great idea.

Nippers in the Orchard

IN the corner of old maps, one used to find the declaration "Here be dragons." This image, being a map of Faery, declares: "Here be nippers." In fact, here be several little nippers, two knockers, and one late blight.

Orchards have always been magical places, haunted by many spirits. In Somerset, the spirit of the oldest tree was known as **Apple Tree Man**; he was propitiated with songs and cider to maintain fertility. Yorkshire orchards were haunted by a fearsome bogey called **Awd Gogge**, who frightened children but protected the orchard fruit before the harvest. The apple tree is an ancient symbol of the *axis mundi*, or the center of life—thus orchards are a natural gateway into the faery realm and one always finds many faeries there.*

Here it is autumn in the apple orchard. The **Apple Tree Men** look on while the first frost nips their precious fruit. This is a faery time, for Halloween approaches; the old year is ending and the Celtic new year is about to begin. The **Trooping** faeries prepare to move on to their winter home. The **Apple Queen** also prepares, wearing the blossom crown of her youth. She remembers the warmth of the summer sun but does not regret its passing. She has nurtured her offspring, seen their promise fulfilled, and now she is ready to move on to the deeper levels of winter. Through the cold dark months, the **Apple Queen** will regenerate and prepare for spring. She is calm. Her work is done now. The faeries around her are busy, for what was given must now be taken back. The faery blights have come out to play: apples, mildewed by faery sneezes, begin to rot, mold, and decay. These blights might seem destructive, but the withering of the physical allows the full growth of the spirit. The death of worn-out ways of thinking regenerates into something new.

*The apple, to the Celts, was a fruit of fertility, immortality, and renewal. Apples held reincarnating souls in their magical Cauldron of Regeneration—a myth invoked when we bob for apples in a tub at Halloween. The apples of immortality were the food of the gods in northern Europe, and the apple of **Prince Ahmed** in the* Arabian Nights *was known to cure any disease. The apple tree is the central tree of heaven in the tales of the Iroquois tribe; likewise, in Romania, heaven rests on a giant apple tree with its root deep in the Underworld, the home of the faery **Magdalina**. In Arthurian lore, **Sir Lancelot** falls asleep under an apple tree and is spirited away by faery women. On the enchanted Isle of Apples (also known as Avalon), **Morgana le Fay** and a circle of faery queens hold **King Arthur** as he lies sleeping, healing, and preparing to return.*

A Hobyah

This **hobyah** is the terrifying bogeyman that children think lives in the closet—but actually he exists only through the collection of our fears. The **hobyah** thrives on fear, getting stronger and stronger until we face him. He is a sham—a tiny fear blown up all out of proportion—and the smallest positive thought will banish him. All of Faeryland knows this, and none is afraid of him.

Barca, the Snagger

A particularly troublesome faery, the **Snagger** is dangerous to travelers, ripping and tearing their clothes. He also appears on trains and airplanes, where he damages the luggage. He takes great delight in putting runs in stockings and pulling off buttons. He is especially fond of the moment when one gets into or out of a taxi. The classic way to banish the **Snagger** (or indeed any faery or faery spell) is to turn your coat inside out and wear it that way. I find this invariably works. The faery is gone—and so, inexplicably, are most of the people around me.

The Fideal

By the reed-choked edges of lonely lakes, the **fideal** wanders through the twilight longing for a lover. Her song is sad yet irresistibly seductive. Her kiss is cold, tasting of earth. Her hands caress you, hold you, pull you down and down into chill waters. You would happily lie with her forever, wrapped in her watery embrace—but she's gone. She has returned to the dark lakeshore, and you are forgotten.

The **fideal** sings as she walks through the reeds, calling out to her next lover . . . leaving you down in the water's cold depths, eyes unseeing, weeds in your mouth.

Pishogue Pooka

The untrustworthy prince of pishogues* weaves spells to bemuse our senses and confuse our judgment. He is a master of the arts of illusion and delusion, holding up a distorting mirror to reveal the bad in the good and the good in the bad.

Pishogue is the Irish name for faery glamour.

The Soul Shrinker

(right) The **Soul Shrinker** is the progenitor of intolerance and meanness. It provokes malicious gossip and causes us to be disparaging of others. Victims of the **Soul Shrinker** blame everyone else for their troubles, taking no responsibility themselves. Slowly, secretly, moment by moment, with each mean word or unkind thought, this faery works at the deepest levels. As it grows, it diminishes our souls, shrinking and constricting them, squeezing until they are tight and shriveled. Don't become one of the unfortunate victims of this destructive creature. If you detect his foul influence in your words or deeds, banish him from your life.

Black Annis the Blue-faced Hag

There is a chill wind blowing. Bolt your windows and bar the door, for **Black Annis** is about. This highly dangerous faery hag grabs children through open windows and takes them back to her lair to devour them. When horrid **Black Annis** is hungry, her howls can be heard for miles.

Bodach

(above) This shadowy male figure comes down the chimney and is up to no good.

Death

(right) She is, perhaps, the most feared of all faeries. The Irish know her as the **banshee**, a faery woman who keens and wails in the night, foretelling death. In Scotland, she's the **Washer at the Ford**, washing the grave clothes of those about to die. Her shadowy figure appears to each one of us at some point in our lives, bearing an irresistible summons from another world.

Sometimes we can refuse the call for a while, but eventually we must follow. She holds out a vision of our past. Does it shine with joy? Or is it clouded by too many things we neglected to do? It's too late to make changes now. The **Death Faery** awaits, ready to lead us into a future of our own making. Now is the dreaded moment. We must take her hand. It is time to go.

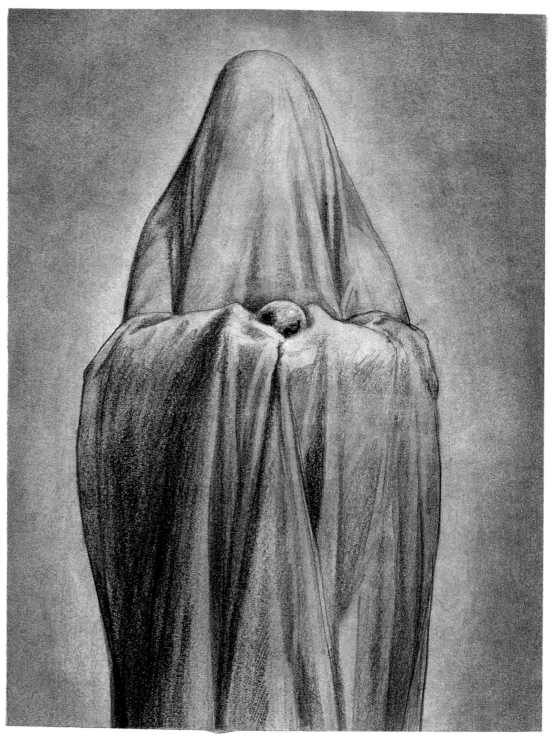

The Red Rager

Small and barely noticeable, this faery lurks in dark recesses, surreptitiously gnawing at us with its venomous little teeth. Then suddenly its color changes to vivid red and it pounces. *Whatever possessed me?* we say afterward. *Something took hold of me. Something came over me.* That something was the **Red Rager**, or **Anger Faery**. It takes wicked pleasure in releasing uncontrolled rage and violent passions. Its twisted form takes us over and we find we're no longer in control. All that is rational and reasonable is devoured by the ravings of this faery, who leaves us in thrall to the darkest forces of Faeryland. "Once bitten, twice shy" is a truism appropriate to dealing with this unwelcome presence. Be constantly vigilant for the first infuriating nips of faery teeth. Possession by the **Red Rager** becomes more virulent the longer it goes on. Compassion is his enemy and keeps him from growing large.

The Sink Faery

This malodorous creature lives down the drain.

Pixie Pincher

(immediately below) Once she was the bane of idlers and sluts (whom she would pinch "blue as bilberries"), but now all of us are at risk from the **pixie pincher**. Any unaccountable bruising will be this pixie's work.

Computer Glitch

(bottom) Who hasn't felt this faery's touch, causing computers to crash, calculators to jam, and bringing darkness to digital screens? I know I have⸗.

The Foul Faery

(above) Of all the creatures spawned by the dark side of Faery, this is one of the most abhorrent. Oozing out of the shadows, it slowly overwhelms its victim, coating all it touches with a sticky web of lies and deceit. This faery hisses in our ear, coaxing us into secretly destructive behavior: covert betrayals, furtive abuse, and violence behind closed doors. The **Foul Faery** thrives in the dark of the unspoken and is banished by the light of truth⸗.

A PERFIDIOUS POOK

THE BIGOT BOGEY

THE BULLY BOGEY

The Bully Bogey

This vicious **bogey** loiters in lonely places and sullenly waits for his prey. His fetid breath inspires brutality and oppressive actions. This **bogey** is the manipulative creature whispering in the ear of all bullies. His contagious influence is felt from schoolrooms to boardrooms to government offices.

The Bigot Bogey

(overleaf) This rancid creature leaps from nowhere with sharp talons and stiff fingers clutching its victims' back, riding them, urging them to spout intransigent dogma. Its harsh voice croaks in their ear, encouraging self-righteousness and fanaticism. The cold tight embrace of the bogey constricts attitudes, producing a rigid narrow-mindedness that excludes all other possibilities. It is one of the most reviled of creatures, even by faeries themselves, for it spawns all that is contrary to the faery faith. An openness of heart is this faery's downfall, and an openness of mind breaks its power. Faeries show us flow and the possibilities of change. They show us clarity and insight and the fact that everything is connected and we are all a part of one another'.

A Perfidious Pook

(overleaf) This false faery manipulates humans into pretense and hypocrisy, inspiring lies and all things false so that they seem plausible and worthy. It throws a glamour over deceit.

A Little Carpet Rucker

Queen of the Bad Faeries

HERE in the light of the waning moon is the **Queen of the Bad Faeries**. In Scotland she is known as **Nicnivin, Elph Queine of the Unseelie Court**. In Germany she's **Berchta**, leading the savage dogs of the Wild Hunt. In Spain she is the **Queen of the Estantigua,** the ancient host of spirits, telling all she meets: "Travel by day, for the night belongs to me." Her domain is the night. She rules over dusk and darkness, shadows and shades. **The Dark Queen**'s power emanates from the dark side of the moon. Much is secret and hidden here, cloaked by dark and illusion. Out of the gloaming beckons the faery woman whose enchantments create madness. An Irish banshee wails her death song, echoed by **La Llorona**, her baleful cousin in the American West. **Black Annis**, the wretched blue-faced hag, sits and grinds her long white teeth. **Hobgoblins** and **bogles** torment the ghostly black dogs who haunt dark country lanes. The human dead are ambassadors to the court of this dark faery queen, for the mounds that faeries inhabit were burial mounds in centuries past.

But every shroud has a silver lining. All things must die to be reborn. The transformative power of Faery turns muck into magic, dross into shining gold, black despair into crystalline joy. Just as life grows out of death, good can grow from those things we call bad. The **banshee** cry foretells change, not death. Blue-faced hags, if we pass the test and embrace them, turn into beautiful women—or perhaps it's not the hags who change, but merely our vision of them. In Irish folklore, hags were once revered as powerful wisewomen, credited with building the ancient cairns and Ireland's sacred mountains.

In the darkness the seeds of good germinate, unfold, grow upward toward the light. Faeryland is the land of paradox: in light there is darkness; in darkness, light.* You will find no absolute evil here within the **Dark Queen**'s realm, for she is a queen of nature, a force of nature, formed from the dreaming earth. True evil exists only in the shadow of man, when he turns his back to the light.

*A blue note: The blue hue permeating the **Dark Queen**'s realm is a mystic color, indicating nobility (blue blood) and deep emotion (blue moods, singing the blues). The color informs us that we are in a special time (once in a blue moon) or that the image carries information (a blueprint). Lighter blues indicate higher spirituality; deeper blues lead us downward into the mysteries of the unconscious.

faeries express the hidden, vibrant life of the natural world

Faeries express themselves with high seriousness and few human

faeries are
resistant to
all definitions

faeries say that there is nonsense in dogma, and sense in nonsense

called the sukuyan, for if she gets one look at herself, the frightened creature quickly runs away.

Turning your coat, socks, or pockets inside out, or standing on your head, or saying things backward puts you on equal terms with the faeries, and they no longer have you in their power. Many faeries cannot penetrate a furze hedge or barrier; most faeries will not be able to cross the threshold of a church. Some faeries cannot cross over running water—but this is a risky remedy, for in other instances crossing running water leads straight into Faery.

The best charm for protection from the faeries is, undoubtedly, cold iron. Pins in a pincushion hung behind a door or a knife in the doorjamb will bar their entry, just as a smoothing iron under the bed prevents abduction during the night. When entering Faeryland it is wise to stab a knife into the door so it cannot be shut again; then you can return home safely. A pocketful of rusty nails can also protect against pixies who would lead you astray. When an animal dies, a nail stuck into its carcass prevents its flesh from being gnawed by sharp little faery teeth.

Cows seem to be particularly susceptible to faery mischief. Bells hung around their necks traditionally kept bovine botherers away. In Ireland, gorse was burned on Midsummer's Eve to protect cattle and crops. After milking, milkmaids used to make the sign of the cross on the side of the cow to protect it from the faeries' attention. When they were churning, a small burning coal under the churn guarded against spoiled butter. Country folk also left small pieces of butter as gifts for the faeries, as well as any spilled milk. In Russia, the goodwill of the chlevnik (cattle spirit) was needed to protect the cows from harm. This faery was propitiated with food and vodka, and his preferences in the matter of cattle color were acceded to.

Soap was the traditional offering left out for the bannick, a Russian spirit who lived under the toilet seat—just in case he or any other household faeries might care to bathe. (Without such an offering it was considered dangerous to visit the bathroom at night.) In Germany, a jug of beer was left out each night for cellar-dwelling kobolds; in Japan, rice wine appeased spirits and wandering ghosts who might do harm. It is still a good idea to leave water and food out at night for your local faeries' refreshment. In the morning the food will still be there, but the goodness will have been extracted. This is true soul food, reminding us that faeries need to be nurtured by gifts of the spirit. Conversely, Faery Food looks dazzling and delicious to us, but in reality it is only weeds or leaves or moss concealed by glamour, reminding us that surface appearance can hide the truth of things.

mystic, mournful rhythm seem to touch the deepest chords of feeling." Yet as we listen to the songs of Faery, we must not forget they can be dangerous. It is not wise to linger too long or to join the faeries in their moonlit revels. A single night of dancing with the faeries can be a transcendent experience—but you might wake on a cold hillside to find that a hundred years have passed and your life has crumbled into dust.

Protection Against the Faeries

IT is well known that faeries love to steal human babies, substituting a changeling—a faery form that bears the appearance of the child but is actually a wizened old goblin or a rotten piece of wood. Up to the last century in the British Isles, midwives would protect newborns by blessing them with three drops of water (one for peace, one for wisdom, and one for purity) as they recited these words:

To aid thee from the fays
To guard thee from the host
To aid thee from the gnome
To shield thee from the spectre.

Protection could also be gained by burning leather or bindweed in the room, or sprinkling the milk of a cow that has eaten pearlwort, or hanging rowan twigs in the form of a cross over the cradle, or leaving iron tongs inside the infant's bed. (Many faeries loathe iron.) In Cambodia, rice wine was sprayed over the body of children tormented by bad spirits. Cambodian parents could also call upon the arak, beneficent household faeries, for protection against disease and the attentions of malign spirits. In West Africa, food was left in the corner of the house for any wandering spirits so that they would not be tempted to enter the bodies of children to gain their nourishment. In Armenia, children seven months old were particularly at risk of abduction by the āls (half-animal, half-human demons). To keep the āls at bay, the infants were surrounded by items made of iron throughout the seventh month. In Russia, a circle was drawn around the beds of small children with the point of an iron-handled knife to keep them safe from old Nocnitsa, the dreaded night hag. Although children were most at risk, adults were also prone to faery abduction—particularly musicians, artists, smiths, midwives, pretty girls, and handsome youths.

Various traditional methods can guard against faery abduction (or any unwanted faery attention), such as carrying or wearing certain plants: hazel wands, rowan (or mountain ash), Saint-John's-wort, daisy chains. In France, flaxseed is spread on the floor to rid a house of goblin infestation. In Mexico, tobacco smoke is believed to chase away the chanekos (little people). In Trinidad, a mirror is used to protect against a spirit

faeries trip you up to give you a new perspective on the world

faeries hide what you want and reveal what you need

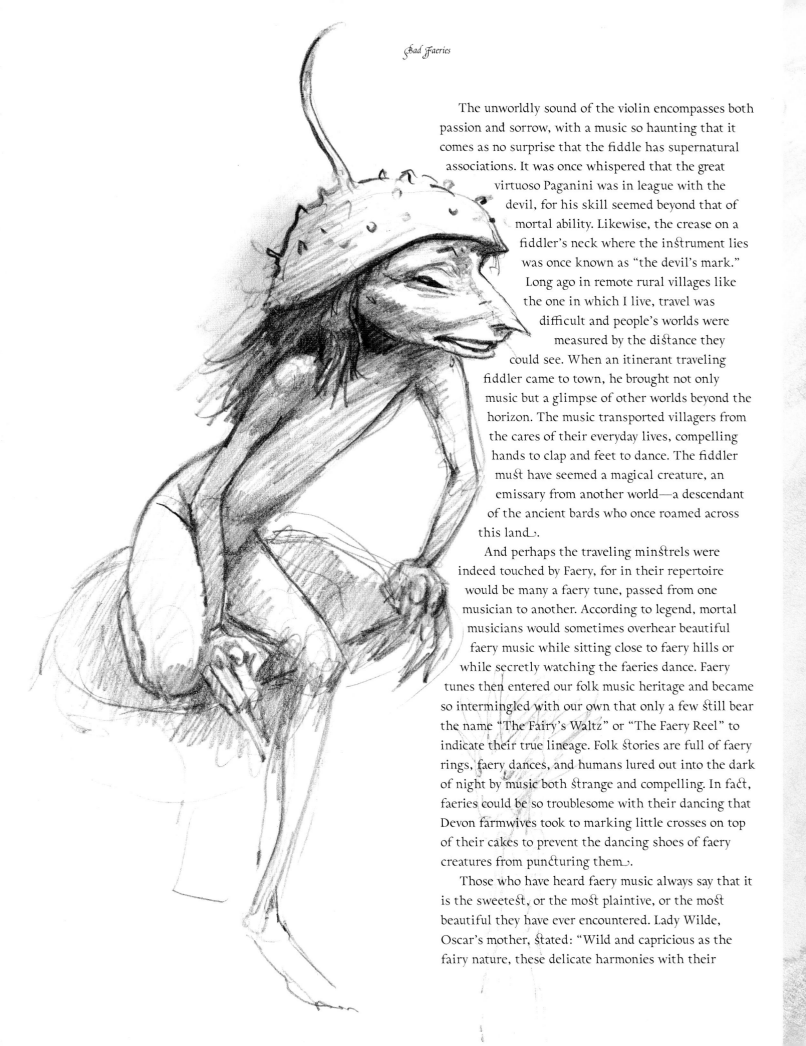

The unworldly sound of the violin encompasses both passion and sorrow, with a music so haunting that it comes as no surprise that the fiddle has supernatural associations. It was once whispered that the great virtuoso Paganini was in league with the devil, for his skill seemed beyond that of mortal ability. Likewise, the crease on a fiddler's neck where the instrument lies was once known as "the devil's mark." Long ago in remote rural villages like the one in which I live, travel was difficult and people's worlds were measured by the distance they could see. When an itinerant traveling fiddler came to town, he brought not only music but a glimpse of other worlds beyond the horizon. The music transported villagers from the cares of their everyday lives, compelling hands to clap and feet to dance. The fiddler must have seemed a magical creature, an emissary from another world—a descendant of the ancient bards who once roamed across this land.

And perhaps the traveling minstrels were indeed touched by Faery, for in their repertoire would be many a faery tune, passed from one musician to another. According to legend, mortal musicians would sometimes overhear beautiful faery music while sitting close to faery hills or while secretly watching the faeries dance. Faery tunes then entered our folk music heritage and became so intermingled with our own that only a few still bear the name "The Fairy's Waltz" or "The Faery Reel" to indicate their true lineage. Folk stories are full of faery rings, faery dances, and humans lured out into the dark of night by music both strange and compelling. In fact, faeries could be so troublesome with their dancing that Devon farmwives took to marking little crosses on top of their cakes to prevent the dancing shoes of faery creatures from puncturing them.

Those who have heard faery music always say that it is the sweetest, or the most plaintive, or the most beautiful they have ever encountered. Lady Wilde, Oscar's mother, stated: "Wild and capricious as the fairy nature, these delicate harmonies with their

Faery Glamour

A glamour, or glamer, is a spell, a juggling of sight that creates an alluring illusion. These false, seductive images mask rather than reveal the truth about Faeryland—and the world around us. Beautiful things disguised by glamour seem ugly; ugly things seem beautiful. Seductions by glamorous faery women seem life enhancing yet lead to despair. Conversely, a loathsome, toothless hag might actually be a lovely faery beneath the false illusions of glamour, and if you bravely kiss her she will turn back to her proper shape.

A glamour can last an hour, a day, a year, or even a lifetime. In its grip, we live in a world unrelated to physical reality, unable to perceive what's true within ourselves and others. In daily life we encounter many people who seem to be caught under a glamour, blinded by the allure of money, physical beauty, celebrity, or the glitter of bright, hollow ideas. A faery glamour can manifest itself as a reluctance to grow up and to face up to things, or a deep unwillingness to see life as it really is. A life lived under a faery glamour is a life filled with missed chances and regrets. When the spell ends and the glamour falls from your eyes, it may be too late.

Some people attracted to Faeryland are blinded by a common illusion: they are willing to see only a sweet and magic-sparkly view of the faeries, missing the deeper, darker, profound power of all things fey. Do not be led astray. Ground yourself in the physical world after an encounter with Faery. Remember that each journey to Faery is complete only when we come home again and make human sense of faery nonsense, passing on or making use of whatever we have learned.

Approached with open eyes and ears as well as a healthy dose of caution, a faery encounter can be experienced without grave mishap. But beware of all things that sparkle too brightly. Make sure that gold is really gold . . . and not just bits of glamorized leaves and dross under a faery's spell.

Faery Music

Music is a delight to the faeries and a sure way to capture their attention. Musicians are particular favorites of theirs—particularly those who play the Celtic harp or the violin. More than one modern folk musician can describe a faery encounter, even if they then laugh it off or put it down to too much drink.

Folklore abounds with tales of faery harpers seducing mortal maids with irresistible music. In old folk ballads we find Thomas the Rhymer, a Scottish harper of great renown, who is spirited away to entertain the Faery Queen for seven years. When the faeries steal the beautiful wife of the mortal King Orfeo, he goes to their hall disguised as a wandering minstrel, a harp upon his back. The Faery King rashly grants him whatever prize he requests. King Orfeo demands the return of his wife, to the faeries' chagrin.

faeries lead us astray to show us the way

from Widecombe, high up on the moor, back home to my village. Suddenly the Wild Hunt was upon him. Jet-black hounds with glowing eyes were baying all around him, barely under the control of the weird Huntsman who led them. The man boldly asked what it was they hunted. Wordlessly, the Huntsman threw him a small bundle, gathered his dogs, and rode away. The man hurried across the moor, clutching the bundle. Only in the candlelight of his home could he see that he held the dead body of his own child.

The faeries take great umbrage at interruptions and interference. There are many accounts of men and women punished for interrupting faery revels, chopping down faery bushes and trees, or otherwise giving offense. A farmer in Cornwall decided to steal the stone basin from the local pisky's well, with the intention of turning it into a nice new water trough for his pigs. He chained the stone to two oxen and pulled it to the top of a steep hill—whereupon the stone broke free of the chains, rolled downhill, made a sharp turn left, and settled back into its place. One of the oxen died on the spot and the hapless farmer was struck lame.

Like any supernatural encounter, meeting a faery—even one who is gentle and benign—is never a comfortable experience. But to meet one of the dark creatures from the shadowed depths of the faery Otherworld can be frightening indeed. As you travel into the faeries' domain, it is best to be wary of things unseen and of the music that lures you into the woods. And always treat faeries with courtesy. You don't want to make them angry.

Faery Defects

TRADITIONALLY one often finds that faeries, even the most beautiful, will have some striking defect of form. Some are hollow backed or elongated; some have goat's or lion's feet. Some brownies have fingers jointed together or lack proper noses and mouths. Heads, hands, and feet are often large in proportion to the rest of the body. This is due to the plastic nature of a faery's astral body, which is often in a state of transition. Distortions, irregularities, strange proportions, and shape-shifting flux are all distinct faery traits.

Sometimes a lack of emotion is a faery's most notable defect. This indicates that its attention is elsewhere, focused on its own Otherworldly concerns—or else that it is only a small fragment of a larger consciousness. Faeries are not complete in themselves but embody aspects of nature's soul. As such, they reach completion and wholeness only by integration with natural phenomena and one another. Faeries belong to a world where each creature is linked in some way with every other. Individually, they can seem imperfectly formed and incomplete, for each is a part of the whole.

The Dark Side of Faery

Faeries, like humans, are bound to nature and thus reflect its capacity for destruction as well as creation. Having studied faeries for many years now, I've learned that the dark side of these creatures must never be ignored—for it is extremely powerful, with the raw power of a natural force.

Numerous indeed are the folktales that remind us of the dangers of Faery and of the many treacherous creatures the unwary traveler might encounter in that realm. The lamia is a seductive faery woman who gives men pleasure beyond their wildest dreams, but she sucks their life's vitality and leaves an empty husk behind. The lovely nixies who dwell in the rivers may be enchanting to look upon, but humans who spy on nixies at play are pulled into the water and drowned. The wail of the banshee foretells a death; Jack-in-Irons assaults travelers on lonely roads; and the Red-caps earned their names by dyeing their hats in human blood. At certain times of year (such as All Hallows' Eve) it is wise to stay safely within doors, for the Faery Host goes riding across the land hunting for souls. Scottish legends have a name for this dark side of Faery: they call it the Unseelie Court—and woe to any woman or man who underestimates its dangers.

Where I live, on Dartmoor, we are haunted by apparitions of sinister black dogs—a typical faery form. (Arthur Conan Doyle's *Hound of the Baskervilles* was written near here and is based on one of these dark apparitions.) One stormy night a man was walking

Faery Blights

FAILED crops were once blamed on the mischief or malice of faeries. The Irish potato famine of 1846–47 was attributed by some country people to disruptions caused by various factions in Faeryland, and witnesses reported seeing great faery battles in the sky above the blighted fields. In those days, faeries were still known to have a profound effect on our physical and psychic well-being. They were known as the bestowers of special gifts and curses at the cradle: talents and handicaps, and luck both good and bad.

Childhood wasting illnesses were often attributed to the faeries. Sometimes children were stolen by the faeries and sickly replicas left in their place. These changelings wasted away and died, buried under the child's name, while the real child remained a prisoner in Faeryland. In Armenia, the āls were spirits of disease blamed for causing miscarriages, blinding unborn children, and stealing infants away. In Persia the devs stole newborn babes and left withered changelings in their beds; in Japan it was the bakemono (goblins); in Malaysia, the bajang, an evil spirit in the form of a polecat. In West Africa, spirits called the abiku were known to be particularly dangerous to children. Voraciously hungry, the abiku searched for vulnerable young bodies to enter in order to obtain food and drink, at which point the child's own strength and health quickly deteriorated. In Germany, the pilwiz (an evil creature with a sickle on his big toe) was given food on Walpurgis Night to protect children from harm.

Many adult illnesses have also been attributed to faeries and spirits. The term "stroke" comes from Elf Stroke (or the Touch): invisible faery fingers stroking their victims into seizures. Amadán, the faery Fool of Irish folklore, was particularly feared in this regard; also known as the Stroke Lad, his touch caused crippling injuries and permanent paralysis. "Touched" is also a word still used today to refer to madness. The arrows of Faery, called Elf Shot, created invisible wounds with fatal results, a phenomenon used to explain a variety of mysterious ills. A faery's glance or look could induce a state of trance, forgetfulness, even coma. The Faery Blast was an ill wind blowing nobody any good. Deformities, barrenness, cramps, slipped discs, and rheumatism were all considered faery work, while blindness could be caused by an angry faery spitting in your eye. Consumption was the result of nocturnal abductions to faery mounds. Squints and sneezes, pimples and poxes were all evidence of faery influence, and cures were as various as ripping your shirt or washing in south-running water. A cure from 1574 recommends "oyle of bay on a linnen cloth" laid upon the afflicted place. Moss from the water of a millstream, salt poured on the table, and the Lord's Prayer said three times were each considered efficacious against the faeries.

Yet only a proper and stable relationship with the faeries could truly effect a cure or ward off such faery blights altogether. When treated in a respectful manner, the faeries brought people into a balanced relationship with the workings of their own bodies and the mysteries of nature.

Danger of Death

THE faeries take great umbrage at interruptions and interference. There are many accounts of men and women for whom death is the ultimate punishment for interrupting faery revels or chopping down faery bushes and trees. In a typical story, an old man recalled going berry picking when he was a boy along with his brother and a female cousin. Suddenly they came upon a group of faeries dancing. A faery woman, dressed in red, rushed forward and hit the girl across the face. The frightened children ran back home, but when they reached the house the girl dropped dead.

faeries are profound ~ profoundly annoying

inflicting various harms and ills on man and beast alike. In *The Fairy Faith in Celtic Countries* (1911), the American folklorist W. Y. Evans Wentz asserted that the faery race had the power to destroy half the human race yet refrained from doing so out of ethical considerations. Lady Gregory (the Irish folklorist, playwright, and patron of W. B. Yeats) held the faeries in rather less awe; she claimed they were merely capricious and mischievous, like unruly children.

In modern life, we are not free from the plagues and torments of bad faeries. They make their presence known to us through all manner of disruptions, from minor daily irritations to serious problems affecting our health and well-being.

Among the minor faery mischief makers are ones we're all familiar with: the snagger, whose sharp claws attack women's stockings before they leave the house; the various spotters and stainers, who leave the grubby evidence of their manifestation on a freshly laundered blouse or tie, usually right before that important business meeting; the sneaker sneaker, who always waits until Monday morning, when the kids are late for the bus, to silently sneak away with a shoe. We've all had personal tongue tanglers, and sudden stark panics, and gloominous dooms, and moments when afterward we say: *Good heavens, whatever possessed me?* The faeries have possessed you, tangling your words, your thoughts, your feet, or your fate. These capricious creatures have been known as frairies, feriers, ferishers, fear-sidhe (faery men), and fearies—a whole race of beings known to block potential and clarity of thought. They hide behind tiny irritations and lurk within our daily disasters. In more serious guise, they're the faery blights whose touch can cause depressions, addictions, compulsions, and moments of dark despair.

It is the nature of faeries to be unruly, chaotic, disruptive, subversive, confusing, ambivalent, paradoxical, and downright frustrating. Yet even these bad interferences serve an important function. They remind us of the value of connection, wholeness, and openness by holding a mirror up to us and showing us the opposite. Bad faeries, from the small sock stealers to the larger creatures of gloom and doom, are (like all faeries) expressions of nature and of our own deepest selves. They are manifestations of psychic blocks, distortions, and unresolved emotions; they give form and personality to negative forces and abstractions. They nip and prod us, asking for simple acknowledgment of their presence in our lives, insisting that we take notice of them—the first step to healing or change.

It cannot be denied that sickness, madness, and even death have been reported in many old tales concerning encounters with the shadow side of Faeryland—yet the same faeries have also been known to give gifts, guidance, and aid to the needy, and to heal mortals of illnesses both physical and psychological. I believe no faery is completely good or bad, but fluidly embodies both extremes. Any faery can be either one or the other in his or her equivocal relationship with us. They change with circumstance, with whim, and with motivations far beyond our human ken. Their actions and reactions generally work toward engaging us at deeper and deeper levels of consciousness—insisting we be conscious of them, of ourselves, and of the world around us. They can become quite angry and disruptive if we're not awake and paying attention—particularly if they feel they've not been properly acknowledged.

The bad faery in the story "Sleeping Beauty" is one example: she is angry because she has been neglected—overlooked at the christening feast. Yet her wickedness initiates the events that lead to the princess's final transformation. Could this have been her intent all along, beyond the guise of wickedness? When dealing with the faeries it is wise to remember that things aren't always as they first appear. What seems to be bad behavior might have a deeper, underlying reason.

Despite our tendency to split the world into good and bad, right and wrong, light and dark, we must remember that in truth (and in the faery realms) such divisions are not always cleanly cut. Each contains a piece of the other, holding the world in tension and balance. And the shape-shifting denizens of Faery can appear wearing either face.

ALTHOUGH people nowadays tend to think of faeries as gentle little sprites, anyone who has encountered faeries knows they can be tricksy, capricious, even dangerous. Our ancestors certainly knew this. Folklore is filled with cautionary tales about the perils of faery encounters, and in centuries past there were many places where people did not dare to go a-hunting for fear of little men.

The idea that the world is full of spirit beings both bad and good is one we find in the oldest myths and tales from cultures the world over. In ancient Greece, the Neoplatonist Porphyry (c. 232–c. 305 A.D.) wrote that the air was inhabited by good and bad spirits with fluid bodies of no fixed shape, creatures who change their form at will. These were certainly faeries. Porphyry explained that the bad spirits were composed of turbulent malignity and created disruptions whenever humans failed to address them with respect. The Romans acknowledged the presence of faery spirits called the Lares, who, when venerated properly at the hearth (the heart) of the household, protected the home and family. The Lares were ruled over by their mother, Larunda, an earth goddess and faery queen. The Roman bogeymen were the Lemures, dark spirits of the night. They had all the traits of bad faeries and had to be placated by throwing black beans at them while turning one's head away.

In northern Europe, the maggots emerging from the dead body of the giant Ymir transmuted into light and dark elves—light elves inhabiting the air, dark elves dwelling in the earth. Persian faeries, known as the peri, were creatures formed of the element of fire existing on a diet of perfume and other exquisite odors. The bad faeries of Persia, called the dev, were forever at war with the peri, whom they captured and locked away in iron cages hanging high in trees. Other faery creatures, both benevolent and malign, appear in tales from many far-flung lands: the laminak of Basque folklore, the grāma-devatā of India, the jinn of Arabia, the hsien of China, the yumboes of West Africa, the underhill people of the Cherokee . . . and numerous other spirits who have both plagued and aided humankind since the world began.

In the early seventeenth century, a certain Dr. Jackson held the view that good and bad faeries are simply two sides of the same coin: "Thus are the fayries from difference of events ascribed to them, divided into Good and Bad, when it is by one and the same malignant fiend that meddled in both, seeking sometimes to be feared, otherwiles to be loved." An English text from the sixteenth century states that "there be three kinds of fairies, the black, the white and the green, of which the black be the woorst"—although in Shakespeare's *The Merry Wives of Windsor* (1602), another group of faeries was added: "Faeries black, grey, green and white," with little indication as to their nature.

In old Scotland, there was no doubt that there were only two groups of faeries: the Gude Fairies and the Wicked Wichts. In the former category was the Seelie Court (the good or blessed court), a host of faeries who were benefactors to humans, giving bread, seeds, and comfort to the needy. These faeries might give secret help in threshing, weaving, and household chores, and were generally kind—but they were strict in their demands for appropriate reparation. The Unseelie Court, by contrast, were fearsome creatures,

Introduction

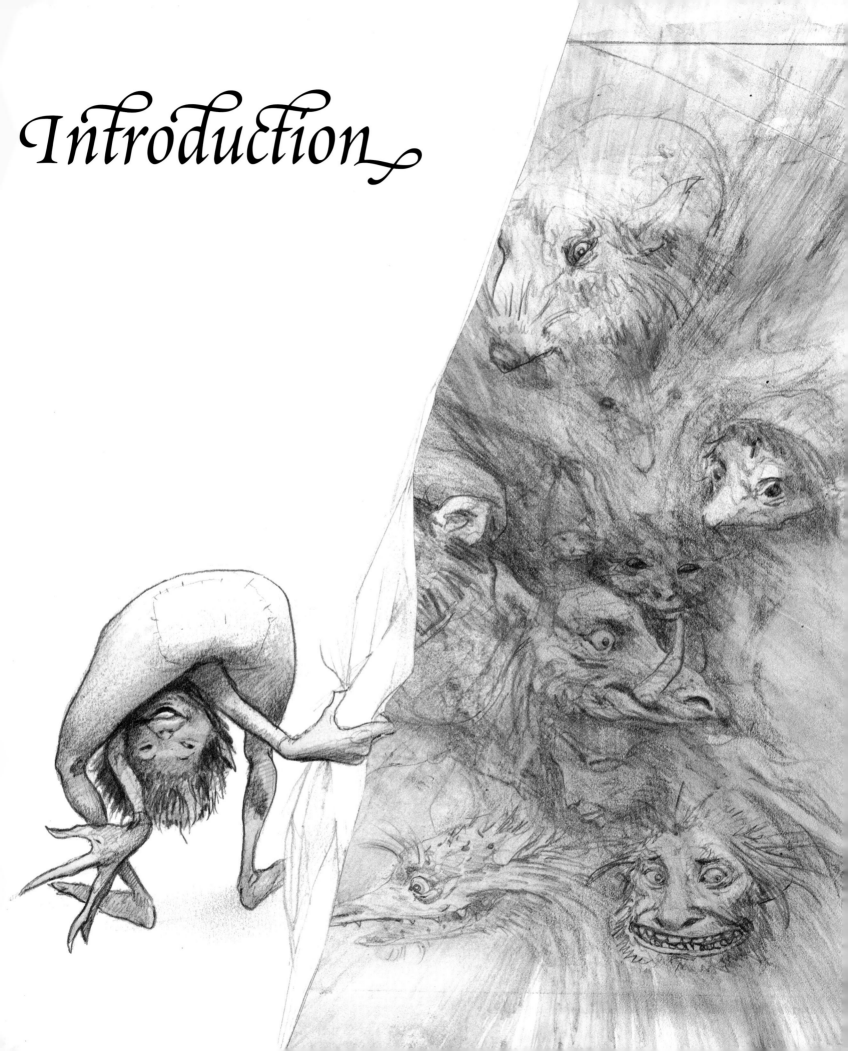

gifts. You'll find them in forests, on mountains, in deserts, on sandy reefs at the edge of the sea; in the gold mist of a country dawn or the silver smoke of an urban twilight; in England and in America . . . and in landscapes throughout the world. Faeries are the inner nature of each land, and a reflection of the inner nature of our souls. They surround me now, as they surround you—you need only the sight to see them.

The pictures in this book all insisted on manifesting themselves on my drawing board. Nothing is made up—these images are direct faery communications. The words I've used to describe the pictures emerged from the same mysterious place, pulsing into and out of focus as though they came to me through distorting glass. This is the way faeries communicate, with high seriousness combined with humor, with symbols, lists, jokes, connections, repetitions, tangents, and deliberate confusions. The smallest figure in the background of a picture might be the most important aspect of all; or an absurd phrase might contain the hidden message the faeries intend. Some faeries demand a complex understanding and mythological erudition; others express themselves elliptically; still others are deceptively direct. Some words I resisted, feeling they were too obscure or simply ridiculous . . . but the faeries insisted, reminding me that not all meanings are meant to be clear at once. Some ideas take time. Some words are designed to lead us on to inner journeys, with truth hidden deep inside them. In Faeryland, that which seems most absurd is often the key to communication with higher spiritual forces. It is a land where wisdom is inseparable from whimsy and where leprechauns dance with the angels.

This is a very personal book in that you, the reader and viewer, are looking through my eyes and my heart into Faery—and yet it's my hope that these images will encourage your own second sight to develop. Joseph Campbell has said that artists are the "shamans and myth-makers" of our modern world. Like Campbell, I believe in the artist as shaman, journeying deep into uncharted inner worlds, then bringing back sensations and visions encountered in that mythic terrain. I see my pictures as maps of the journeys I've taken through the realms of the soul. And I hope that these maps will lead you to find faery pathways of your own.

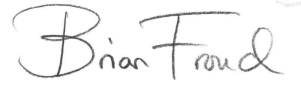

faeries are irrational, poetic, absurd, and very, very wise

In ancient Greece, the word *eidōla* meant image, and *eidōlon* meant soul. Image, then, was a way of understanding and envisioning the soul. This is a book of what I call "imaginosis," or *knowing through image*—a book of images designed to spark self-revelation. Such images grow from my own inner journeys and daily contact with the faeries. By experience I have found them to be irrational, poetic, absurd, paradoxical, and very, very wise. They bestow the gifts of inspiration, self-healing, and self-transformation . . . but they also create the mischief in our lives, wild disruptions, times of havoc, mad abandon, and dramatic change.

Humans have long maintained close daily connections with the faeries. In centuries past, we've acknowledged them by many traditional names: boggarts, bogles, bocans, bugganes, brownies, blue-caps, banshees, miffies, nippers, nickers, knockers, noggles, lobs, hobs, scrags, ouphs, spunks, spurns, hodge-pochers, moon dancers, puckles, thrumpins, mawkins, gally-trots, Melsh Dicks, and myriad others. Just as they have many different names, they appear to us in many different guises. They are shape shifters, highly mutable, for no faery or nature spirit has a fixed body. In their essence, faeries are abstract structures of flowing energy, formed of an astral matter that is so sensitive as to be influenced by emotion and thought. In their most primal form, we perceive them simply as pulsing forces of radiant light, with a glowing center located in the region of the head or heart. (In the more highly evolved faeries, the head and the eyes are more strongly defined.) Responding both to mythic patterns and to human thoughts, these abstract forces delight in coalescing into wings and flowing drapery, taking on shapes that reflect the human, animal, plant, and mineral worlds.

In this book, we explore the nature of faeries in all their various shape-shifting guises. As guardians, guides, godmothers, and muses, the *good faeries* of the twilight realm are agents of self-growth and transformation, embodiments of the healing energies that flow through nature and through ourselves. Both luminous and illuminating, they reveal hidden aspects of our souls.

Yet as centuries' worth of folklore points out, faeries can also be tricksy creatures, delighting in all things irrational, nonsensical, and wickedly absurd. Did you ever wonder why your socks never match or buttered toast always falls facedown? Did your ever wonder what a Pang of Regret looks like? Or a Mild Panic? Here you'll see the faces and forms of the creatures behind these and darker problems—the *bad faeries* who pinch us, nip us, trip us up, and lead us astray. Yet even bad faeries have their gifts to bestow when we understand their contrary natures. By recognizing and naming them, you'll find they can teach you how to spin the straw of your life into gold.

The pictures that follow were inspired by the dynamic, spirited world around me: the faery creatures who have guided, disrupted, enchanted, and plagued my daily life—pushing, prodding, provoking, sometimes tripping me up so that (flat on my back) I can see from a new perspective. They populate my studio, snooze among the books and paints, flit through the windows, nest in the cupboards, play silly pranks, and offer bright

to have captured the imaginations of the greatest number of readers. When I ventured out of my Devon studio to work on projects halfway across the world, people sought me out clutching well-worn copies of the volume. They were of all ages and from all walks of life, but they had one thing in common: an intense relationship with the book and an immense affection for the imagery within. The faeries had entered their lives, and shaped their dreams, and touched their hearts.

It has been twenty years since *Faeries* was published, and in that time I have never stopped my own personal intensive exploration of the faery realm. During these years I met my wife, Wendy, a sculptor and doll maker, on the set of *The Dark Crystal;* our son, Toby, was born; and we moved to a seventeenth-century Devon longhouse built on Saxon foundations. Faery paintings and drawings began to crowd me out of my studio, spilling into the rest of the house alongside my wife's mythic sculptures, woodland masks, and faery dolls. My paintings are not illustrations drawn from specific stories or folklore texts; rather, they are images painted intuitively, springing directly from visions guided by faery muses, a paradoxical mix of chance and intent. As this body of faery imagery grew, I also followed the faeries'

footsteps in the study of world mythology, archetypal psychology, and magical esoterica. Through painting, I discovered much about faery nature in a daily, very personal way—and then found these discoveries echoed in myth, folklore, art, and visionary writings from cultures all around the world.

Faeries was a book that concentrated on the faeries of the past, found in old British tales. *Good Faeries/Bad Faeries* is about the magic in our lives today; it links faeries of the past with faeries of the present and the future. I'd always wanted this book to be more than just a presentation of my faery art. I'd also hoped to address the process of creativity and imagination that enables direct communi-cation with the luminous, living faery realm. In folklore, they say that those who can see the faeries are blessed with *second sight*. Where some people perceive only empty fields, a man or woman with second sight can see a host of faeries dancing in a ring or the shining entrance to a faery hill. Where some notice only an ordinary street of shops or a marketplace, others see faeries in human disguise, paying for market goods with magical coins that will turn into mere stones and leaves when the faeries have gone.

Through painting pictures and listening to the spirit of the beautiful land where I make my home, I have discovered that the second sight is not limited to people in old folktales. We can all learn to have the sight to see the faery world around us. It shimmers in every autumn leaf and lingers in every cool blue shadow; it gives every stone and stream and grove of trees vibrant, animate life. Second sight can also be called *in-sight:* into the faery realms, into the very heart of nature . . . and into the mystical world that lies deep within the human soul.

Preface

ONCE UPON A TIME, I thought faeries lived only in books, old folktales, and the past. That was before they burst upon my life as vibrant, luminous beings, permeating my art and my everyday existence, causing glorious havoc.

Until 1976, I lived in London and worked as an illustrator, creating images to go along with other people's words. Then I moved to a small country village in Devon, along with my friend Alan Lee and his family. As I walked through forests of oak and ivy, across the wild expanse of Dartmoor, among stone circles, Bronze Age ruins, and tumbled stones of old castle walls, I began to hear words and stories whispered by the land itself. I listened to those stories, soaking in the spirit of the land with its wealth of folklore and myth. Together, Alan and I created *Faeries*, a book of pictures and faery lore, which went on to become an international best-seller. This book was considered by many to be a definitive guide to the faery realm . . . but I soon discovered that my journey through the land of Faery had only just begun. I learned that the denizens of that land weren't confined to stories from an age long gone—they were all around me, tangible pulses of energy, spirit, emotion, and light. They took on form as they stepped into my art, cloaked in shapes of nature and myth. I'd attracted their attention while creating *Faeries*, and they weren't finished with me yet.

In the years after the publication of *Faeries* I worked on many other projects, each of them steeped in magic. For Jim Henson, I designed two movies based upon my art: *The Dark Crystal* and *Labyrinth*. I published other books such as *The World of the Dark Crystal*, *Brian Froud's Faerielands*, *Lady Cottington's Pressed Fairy Book*, *Strange Stains and Mysterious Smells*, and *The Goblin Companion* (the last three with Terry Jones of *Monty Python* fame). Yet of all these publications, *Faeries* seemed

The faeries I draw are a spontaneous manifestation
of my relationship with the world.
A normally invisible domain is given form first
of all in my sketchbooks. faerie faces emerge from
the blank white pages as if out of a mist.
A few loose random squiggles are drawn,
and suddenly a complete personality appears,
demanding attention and a name.

Bad Faeries

Brian Froud

Edited by Terri Windling

PAVILION

First published in the United States of America in 1998 by
SIMON AND SCHUSTER EDITIONS, New York in 1998

This edition published in Great Britain in 2004 by
PAVILION BOOKS

An imprint of Chrysalis Books Group

The Chrysalis Building, Bramley Road, London W10 6SP

Copyright © 1998 by Brian Froud

The moral right of the author and illustrator have been asserted

Design and Art Direction by Fiona Andreanelli
and David Costa at Wherefore Art? London

A CIP catalogue record for this book is available from the British Library.

ISBN 1 86205 3022

Printed in Singapore by Imago

4 6 8 10 9 7 5

This book can be ordered direct from the publisher.
Please contact the Marketing Department.
But try your bookshop first.

Bad Faeries

For Wendy